Raw food diet for dogs

Raw food diet
for dogs

The fresh food diet – made easy

by Silke Böhm

Copyright © 2011 Cadmos Publishing Limited, Richmond, UK
Copyright of original edition © 2006 Cadmos Verlag GmbH, Schwarzenbek, Germany
Design: Ravenstein + Partner, Verden
Setting: Das Agenturhaus, Munich

Cover photograph: Sabine Hans
Content photos: Sabine Hans
Translation: Andrea Höfling
Editorial of the original edition: Dr Gabriele Lehari
Editorial of this edition: Christopher Long

Printed by: Westermann Druck, Zwickau

British Library Cataloguing in Publication Data
A catalogue record of this book is available from the British Library.

Printed in Germany

ISBN: 978-0-85788-203-5

Contents

6

Contents

Contents

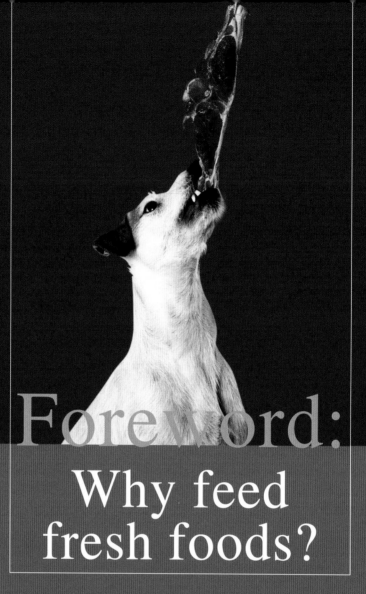

Foreword:
Why feed
fresh foods?

When our Parson Russell terrier Yoda moved in with us in August 2003, the breeder supplied us with a starter packet of dried dog food. Having been a vegetarian for twenty years at first I was glad that dried dog food was available. After the starter pack was nearly used up, I made a few enquiries regarding the subject of diet, and was surprised to see how much the quality varied among the different dog foods on offer. This prompted me to embark on a very extensive research campaign, scouring the internet, forums, books and articles. I spent hours on the phone discussing the composition of the various pellets, croquettes and biscuits with the customer advisors of the different food manufacturers. After a prolonged period of weighing up the pros and cons, I plumped for a brand that I believed would be good for my dog.

There is a huge range of dried dog food on offer. However, the quality varies considerably.

Which vegetables and which types of meat is my dog allowed to eat?

Unfortunately my canine friend had a different opinion. At first he refused to eat it. I however remained determined. After two days Yoda ate the food, but with the proverbial 'gritted teeth'. He was a long way away from leaping up in the air upon hearing me handle the food bowl in the kitchen. Also he never ate the recommended amount. And because Yoda is a dog who tends to be rather too slim than too fat, I began to worry.

One day the owner of Yoda's dog friend Leo pushed a packet of fresh meat into my hand. As I was grating some vegetables for the first time that evening, and mixing them up with the meat, I had more than a few trepidations. A pair of eager dog eyes complete with button nose followed each and every one of my hand movements. Yoda emptied his bowl, and licked it clean until it was shiny. The pure joy of watching the dog eat with a healthy appetite should have convinced me of the advantages of a fresh food diet. But I remained sceptical. After all I am a committed vegetarian! I took up my research once more. After a relatively short period of time all my doubts had vanished; if I wanted to feed this dog in a species-appropriate manner, I would have to feed him fresh food. I started by making menu plans and inquiring about any added ingredients, oils and herbs. It took quite a long time before I arrived at my present routine.

Dog owners easily get chatting to each other, and the subject of diet will soon come up as well. People are usually very interested when I tell them that I feed my dog exclusively with fresh food. I have to answer the same questions I had asked myself at the beginning, and which I had painstakingly researched. These chats tend to centre predominantly on how to adapt the theory for everyday purposes, and how user-friendly it is. This book is a direct result of this; it is a practical introduction to the subject of the fresh food diet for dogs, with tips, advice and practical experience.

Incidentally, many fresh food feeders will feed themselves and their families a lot more healthily after switching to fresh food for the dog. This must be due to the fact that you always have fresh vegetables in the house. I consider this to be a rather positive side effect.

The dog's digestive system

The dog is a carnivore and a direct descendant of the wolf. The wolf – just like our domestic dogs – is in fact an omnivore, even though meat is their preferred food. In their natural habitat wolves don't just eat whole animals, but also plants, such as grasses, berries, herbs, as well as fruit and vegetables.

In order to keep a dog in a way that is appropriate to the species, it is necessary to roughly follow the dietary habits of a wolf. This is due to the fact that there is virtually no difference between the digestive system of a wolf and that of a dog. Although the dog is no longer a predator in the true sense – he does not hunt, but instead gets a bowl put in front of him by his human – his digestive organs are still those of a predator. A good balance of meat and vegetables has to be provided. The wolf's usual prey consists predominantly of herbivores. Due to the fact that the stomach contents – an important source of minerals and vitamins – which we don't normally have access to, are also consumed we have to replace these components by providing a range of well thought out supplements.

Let's begin with the dog's mouth. The carnivore tears smaller pieces of meat from a larger chunk with his front teeth, and breaks them up with his molars. He is, however, not able to grind up the food in the same way as we humans or other herbivores do; our saliva initiates the fermentation process while the food is still in the mouth.

The function of the dog's saliva, which is quite viscous compared with human saliva, is not so much to ferment the food, but rather to aid the passage of fairly large lumps of meat down into the digestive tract. The saliva coats the food like a lubricant and eases its transport into the stomach for further digestion. But first the food passes through the oesophagus. This muscular tube pumps lumps of food into the stomach mechanically. The stomach too is a muscle that is constantly moving during the digestive process in order to mix up the individual food components with digestive juices. The mucous lining of the stomach produces comparatively large amounts of hydrochloric acid which modifies the food in order to facilitate enzymatic processing. A dog's stomach can accommodate considerably more volume of food than a human's for example. In theory it would therefore be possible to feed a healthy, fully grown dog only once a day. In practice it has been shown that feeding smaller amounts of food – divided into two to three portions spread out over the day – reduces the risk of a stomach twist, while at the same time avoiding raised stress levels due to hunger.

The carnivore's stomach continuously passes small portions of food on to the intestines. How much and how often depends on the dog's activities. Because the stomach and gut are at their most active after a meal, causing the dog to be tired, he should be allowed to indulge in a siesta after eating. The rule is that after feeding a dog must not be allowed to engage in any demanding activities for one to two hours. Ideally the interval should be even greater than that. This means that dogs who only get fed once a day should be fed as late in the evening as possible. The food mash is pushed from the stomach into the duodenum. From there the food is moved into the small intestine, followed by the large intestine, at the end of which the

Many dogs like to eat the odd berry during their walks.

This dog is licking his nose after a good meal.

The smaller the pile of dog poo, the more efficiently a dog has digested their food.

dog evacuates the indigestible food components. The smaller the output, the more efficiently the dog has absorbed the food.

And you will see that after being put on a fresh food diet your dog will produce fewer, and above all, smaller piles of poop (which is an advantage for all dog owners in urban situations where clearing up after your dog using small plastic bags is mandatory). A dog's gut is much shorter than a human's relative to their body size. This is typical for predators, who are unable to digest complex carbohydrates due to a shorter gut. Owners of dogs who like to chew on sticks will know this phenomenon – the small bits of wood that the dog swallows whilst chewing on the stick re-emerge unchanged at the other end.

The gut of each and every living being transforms food into components small enough to pass through the gut wall into the blood stream in order to supply the human or the animal organism with the required minerals and vitamins. The dog's mucous lining and digestive enzymes are somewhat more efficient than those of a human. Nevertheless they are not able to break down vegetable matter. The wolf eats the pre-digested stomach contents of his prey. In order to adapt the food to suit the dog's digestive requirements we have to break open the vegetable cells either by cooking them, or, and this would be the preferred option, by pureeing them in order to break open the cells. This is the only way the domesticated successor to the wolf is able make optimal nutritional use of his food, in order to stay healthy and active.

During the digestive process some tiny little helpers are playing an important part. These are enzymes which are produced by the stomach lining and the pancreas. These compounds break down the food components further and further, until they are small enough to be absorbed through the gut wall in order to supply the body with vital substances. In the dog's case, the part of the digestive process involving enzymes only begins once the food has reached the stomach. In humans the enzymatic digestion begins in the mouth. The dog's gut flora contains gut bacteria that are able to synthesise vitamins. Despite this the majority of the vitamins needed have to be absorbed via the diet.

Prejudices

Some concerns regarding a fresh food diet are simply based on old prejudice. The dog food industry likes to encourage this kind of prejudice because they are worried about a decrease in demand for ready-made dog food. Some vets also advise against the feeding of fresh food, because they have not yet looked into the matter thoroughly enough. But there are signs of an increasing trend in favour of feeding fresh food among veterinarians.

The most persistent prejudice, however, must be the idea that dogs who are fed raw meat are more aggressive than dogs fed on ready-made food. Anyone willing to give this matter some thought will quickly realise that this cannot be true. What can possibly be bad about feeding a dog with the same food that their ancestor, the wolf, would eat? Wolves living wild in the forest are not aggressive animals. And even for us humans the trend is increasingly towards getting back to our roots. We strive to eat in a more consciously season-oriented way – in other words, more naturally. But does this mean that our menfolk are striding into the forest with their bows and arrows once again?

'A dog who is fed meat will hunt the animals that he finds daily in his food bowl.' This is a very contradictory prejudice too. Why on earth should he? He has no idea what kind of meat he is being fed. In addition prey animal doesn't smell like its meat, but it has its own scent – as each animal does. Apart from this, there are

An old prejudice: no dog becomes aggressive due to being fed fresh food.

Dogs who are fed fresh food don't go hunting – either in the fields or at the butcher's.

the same way as meat destined for human consumption. This is in accordance with our laws. A meat seller who sells meat contaminated with salmonella or worms would quickly lose their job. In addition salmonella don't represent a danger to a healthy dog, because their stomach acid is much more concentrated than that of a human, and is therefore much better at dealing with these types of germs.

'I can't achieve a diet for my dog that is as balanced as ready-made dog food!' If I could have a penny every time I hear this... . But I assure you; you can do a lot better than that. Or would you knowingly put animal by-products – waste products from the food industry – into your dog's food bowl? I wouldn't even know where to buy something like that. Not to mention artificial colour, preservatives and taste enhancers!

The concern that feeding bones may cause calcium deposits in the gut is an old wives' tale. The dog's stomach acid is very strong and breaks down the bone completely. Also the dog's stomach is equipped for the digestion of meat and bones. What is important to bear in mind, however, is that you must only feed raw bones to a dog. Leftover ones from a barbeque or roast are forbidden for the dog, because they have been warmed up or cooked, and are therefore prone to splintering.

In addition I don't accept the prejudice that fresh food is much more expensive that ready-made food. If you are consistent in treating all leftover vegetable peelings not as rubbish, but

some proportions of meat in ready-made food as well. Would a dog who gets fed ready-made 'lamb with chicken' therefore hunt lambs and chickens?

'Dogs who are fed fresh food will get salmonella or worms.' This of course is a complete fairy tale too. Meat fed to dogs is processed in as a valuable food source for your dog instead, if you buy food seasonally and make a conscious choice where you source your meat from, you can often manage to stay below the cost of a high quality ready-made food.

It does take more time to freshly prepare food from scratch. That much I will admit to. However, as each day passes it takes up relatively less time. And before you know it, the feeding routine becomes more and more automatic, until you hardly notice the extra effort any more. Apart from that, by acquiring a dog I have chosen a rather time-consuming hobby at any rate, and a few extra minutes a day won't kill me. If you were a hobby pilot, you'd expect to carry out your hobby to the best of your abilities as well, and make sure that you were able to land your plane safely, wouldn't you?

Feeding bones does not cause calcium deposits in the gut.

Fresh food –
crisp and fresh into the food bowl!

The feeding of fresh food to dogs is getting ever more popular. Those of us taking a closer look at the subject of dog food will soon realise that the tinned and dried foods on the market do not necessarily contain ingredients that we're happy to feed to our dogs. Grain usually tops the list of ingredients, which means that grain makes up the highest proportion of the contents. Sometimes the various types of grain are listed separately, making them move to the bottom of the list. This means that grain is not listed as a collective item, but, for example, as corn flour, wheat flour, rice flour or oats. In terms of percentages these amounts now appear smaller, and at first sight proportionally less – a little trick deployed by the pet food industry. When you add the separate types of grain together again, they once again make up the largest amount.

What's wrong with that? It's simple: dogs don't need grain as part of a balanced diet. Moreover, grain is often the number one trigger for allergies.

Sure, feeding dried and tinned dog food is a simple affair; a handful or spoonful into the bowl, and all the dog's needs are seemingly catered for. In addition many dogs are able to tolerate the ready-made food quite well.

But if you're dealing with a fussy eater, who doesn't accept the ready-made food, or a dog suffering from allergies, you may be at a loss what to do next. A desperate search begins, trawling the world of commercial ready-made

A virtual firework of vitamins and nutrients: fresh meat and vegetables.

What yummy things will be put in my bowl today?

dog food, whilst opened food sachets pile up in the larder, and rejected tins make their way from the fridge into the rubbish bin. There comes a point when the human 'tin opener' is able to recite the list of ingredients on the food containers by heart, like the poems once memorised in his or her schooldays, and on top of that there's the worry about your dog's health. When things have got to this stage, the idea of feeding fresh meat comes to you almost automatically.

A big obstacle to feeding fresh foods is the seemingly large effort required. But once you have settled into a routine, the extra effort is actually not that extreme. And seeing a happy dog who is licking their bowl clean until it's shiny is ample compensation in any case. Of course feeding fresh food takes up a little more of your time. But bearing in mind the overwhelming advantages of producing your own dog food, you will be happy to make the effort for your best friend, for incidentally to have a dog is the nicest hobby in the world.

Cost is also an important factor in favour of feeding fresh food. Once you have worked out how to source the food locally, and you feed seasonal fruit and vegetables grown locally or nationally, in due course the cost of feeding your dog will fall drastically. Go forth and lobby your friends and neighbours! If you order collectively via the internet or from your local abattoir, you can reduce the cost further.

The equipment - from dough scraper to food processor

In order to set up a routine as soon as possible, it makes sense to acquire some good equipment.

Vegetables have to be cooked or pureed in order to enable your dog's digestive system to break them down. However, raw pureed vegetables contain more vitamins, and are therefore the preferred option. You can also grate the vegetables by hand on a daily basis. But the shavings achieved by grating are still relatively large, which means that the cells are not opened up completely – which they would have to be, if you want your dog to be able to break them down and absorb the nutrients. Because of this all vegetables should be made into a proper puree.

My everyday tip
Freeze a few daily portions of pureed vegetables. This provides you with some emergency rations for hectic moments, when you can defrost them in the microwave. Meat, on the other hand, should never be warmed in the microwave.

The acquisition of a good vegetable blender makes the daily feeding routine considerably easier. There is a huge range of food processors on the market – with regard to the price, have a think which household appliances might also be useful for the family's food preparation. Do you bake a lot of cakes? Then perhaps you ought to think about buying a kitchen machine that can also mix pastry and sponge mixtures. Make a note of all the applications you need and ask your electrical appliances retailer for advice. Make sure that the food processor has enough power to puree even raw carrots. Because you are expecting to use the food processor on a daily basis, it should be as easy to clean as possible. For lesser requirements an upright blender can be used. It fits into even the smallest of kitchens, has a pleasing design, and can be cleaned quickly and easily.

With good equipment feeding fresh food is much easier.

My everyday tip

After giving it a quick swill, fill the appliance with a bit of water and turn it on for a short moment. This helps to wash any leftover bits of vegetable puree out of hard to reach corners.

Once bought, meat should be frozen immediately to make sure that the dog gets fresh food every day.

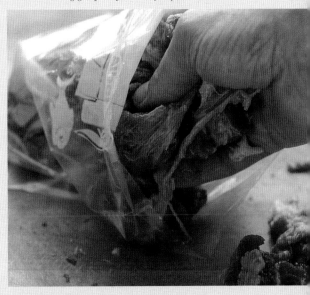

To avoid a loss of quality the meat, once bought, should be frozen on the same day. It is best to divide it into daily rations. This way you can take the portion for the next day out of the freezer the night before and let it defrost slowly in the fridge over night. This leaves only the vegetables to be prepared on a daily basis. In

Plastic containers are useful for freezing food in portions.

Freezer bags, on the other hand, take up less space in the deep-freeze.

> **My everyday tip**
> If you want to freeze meat in freezer bags, it might be worthwhile to buy a welding device for plastic bags. The device sucks out the air, making the meat take up less space.

case you forget to take the meat out of the fridge, you can warm it up relatively gently by immersing it in warm water.

I find that dishwasher-proof plastic containers are very useful for this. In contrast to freezer bags they are not only more ecologically sound, but it also makes making portions less time-consuming. In addition you can 'theme' the containers in the freezer, i.e. stack them according to their contents, and thus create a certain order inside your freezer. After feeding the dog the containers can disappear in the dishwasher, to be re-used on a future occasion.

You can save yourself the bother of laboriously writing out the content on the label by using a points system. For this purpose adhesive dots available from a stationer's can be helpful. Assign a colour to each type of meat, write it down and attach the list to the fridge door with a magnet. Stick the respective dots on the containers and bags, depending on their content. After a very short time you will no longer have to consult the list, because you'll know it by heart. The big advantage is that the other family members will also find it easy to follow the instructions for feeding the dog. An example:

Red: Beef

Green: Lamb

Yellow: Poultry

Blue: Fish

Black: Game

White: Innards or offal (rumen/omasum)

It's a good idea to have some wall-mounted scales near the sink. When buying scales please

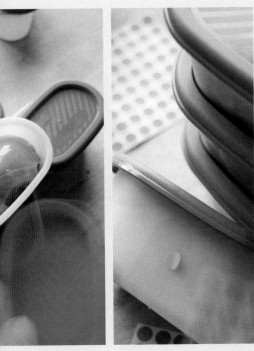

Mark the containers using sticky dots.

Adapting equipment: a liquid soap dispenser for oil and a sugar dispenser for coconut shavings.

make sure that they have a sufficient maximum capacity, depending on the size and weight of the dog. Most kitchen scales available in the high street tend to have a maximum capacity of only two kilograms.

If you don't want to touch the meat, you can use a pair of barbeque tongs for making the meat portions. Latex gloves available from the chemist have also been found to be useful. Any unease regarding the handling of raw meat tends to wear off quite quickly, however.

A liquid soap dispenser (without the soap, of course) is a good device for getting the right amounts of the necessary oils into the food. The soap dispenser should be opaque or kept in a dark cupboard. Many oils lose their beneficial properties due to exposure to sunlight and daylight. Gift labels from the stationers can tell us what's inside. They are decorative and easily changeable when switching to a different type of oil. A sugar dispenser can be used for dispensing powdery substances such as healing earth or grated coconut.

For cleaning the vegetable blender I found a bottle brush, as used in the catering business, most helpful. This way you have no problem cleaning the blender with water and washing up liquid, because often you can't take the blades out of the jar to wash separately.

Equipment costs

Vegetable blender:	from £ 26.00
Freezer tub:	about £ 0.50
Liquid soap dispenser:	about £ 4.50
Sugar dispenser:	about £ 2.00
Bottle brush:	about £ 2.00
Barbeque tongs:	about £ 3.50
Dough scraper:	about £ 0.50

My everyday tip
Second-hand deep-freezes are often available at a relatively low cost from internet portals or in daily newspapers. White goods with small scratches or other slight damage also tend to be cheaper, even when new.

My everyday tip
Buy several dough scrapers at once. They go straight into the dishwasher after use and this way you'll have a fresh one for the next day's scraping of pureed food remnants out of the blender.

For big dogs who eat larger portions, according to their size, it might make sense to think about buying a separate 'dog food deep-freeze' which could be put somewhere such as the cellar. You should pay a lot of attention to the energy efficiency rating. Freezers and fridges can be terrible electricity guzzlers – therefore you should make sure to buy one which is A-rated for energy efficiency. Deep-freezes are better than fridge–freezers, because they use up less electricity and have a greater storage capacity.

You may also have to buy a new food bowl, because the portions will be more voluminous compared to dry dog food.

The everyday routine

Take the required portion of frozen meat out of the freezer compartment in the evening and let it defrost slowly in the fridge overnight. Never close the lids on the containers of meat in the fridge or at room temperature so they are completely airtight. Otherwise unhealthy germs can develop which may harm the dog. The best way is to open the container and place the lid loosely on top. An even better option is a ceramic pot with a lid that had its rubber seal removed, so it is no longer airtight. Put the opened container into the ceramic pot which then goes into the fridge. Take the container out of the fridge the next morning and keep it at room temperature. Put the fruit and vegetables next to it allowing them to warm to room temperature as well. At feeding time put the fruit or vegetables into the vegetable blender adding water, oil and other ingredients. Stir the meat into the mixture – and the dog's dinner is ready to be served.

Cut the vegetables roughly into cubes before putting them into the blender. This is the only way to achieve a thick creamy mixture which the dog is able to digest easily. How small or large you cut the meat for the dog is up to the person feeding the dog. You can serve it in small pieces, similar to goulash, or you can feed it in one big chunk, depending on the human's and the dog's preferences.

This is how appetising dog food can look!

Some dogs like to 'shake to death' the chunk. However, out of consideration for the person whose job it is to clean up afterwards, the meat should be cut into smaller pieces, even if the dog gets a kick out of it otherwise. If you have a garden, you can relocate the feeding of large chunks of meat outdoors. Here the dog can enjoy the 'shaking the prey to death' routine for as long as they like.

Many dogs don't like eating vegetables on their own. In this case the meat can be pureed together with the vegetables. This way, even the fussiest of dogs won't manage to separate out the meat and leave the greens behind. Reservations on the grounds that the dog won't have anything to chew on any more can be neglected. The teeth cleaning and calming effects of gnawing can be achieved through the serving of bone. Another way to 'clean' a dog's teeth is by having them chew rawhide

There are some dogs who don't like raw meat.

chews, windpipes and rumen sticks. Older dogs who don't enjoy their chewing as much as they used to, or animals who only rarely or never get bones to chew on at all have to be taken to the vet regularly in order to get the tartar removed from their teeth. It is also advisable to brush the teeth of such dogs. Special dogs' toothbrushes are available from the vet's surgery.

Some dogs don't like raw meat. In this case you can blanch the meat. You should feed the stock as well, because it contains valuable nutrients. You have to be careful not to serve the dog food that is too hot. In order to convert the dog to eating raw meat, you can gradually reduce the boiling time, until you reach a point where you basically offer them the meat raw. This is a gentle way to introduce a dog to raw food.

If your dog is getting several meals per day, the dog food that has been prepared in advance can be stored in a bowl. Make sure that the container is not sealed completely airtight. Covering the bowl with a saucer will allow some air inside, preventing the development of harmful germs. Don't worry about bad smells. Fresh meat does not smell unpleasant.

Changing to a raw food diet

Some dogs reject raw food at first. As mentioned before, in order to get them used to the new food, the meat can be boiled or fried for a short time, or steamed. With every meal the meat is offered in a slightly more raw state, until it can be fed completely raw.

My everyday tip
You can fill a small perforated plastic container in the house or in the garden, and have the dog search for it. Once he has found the tub, he gets the meat inside. A fun game for dog and human! And this will certainly get him interested in the taste.

In some dogs changing the diet to raw foods can lead to slight detox effects. This can occur immediately or a little later. The detox effect can manifest itself through diarrhoea or constipation, slimy faeces, vomiting, but also through itching and skin problems. Normally the dog will quickly get used to the new diet. If the detox symptoms continue for longer, you must consult a vet in order to exclude other causes. Support the process of changing to a new diet by strengthening the dog's immune system, by feeding them a spring diet (see chapter 'Treating everyday complaints') and by enriching the food with a lot of good herbs.

Changing to the new food regime should be completed within two to three days. During this brief adjustment phase you should make sure that there is a gap of at least twelve hours between feeding dry dog food and fresh food, because the digestion times are very different.

In the case of tinned food, this time gap doesn't necessarily have to be adhered to.

Healthy, stable dogs are usually able to cope with a change in their diet from one day to another. In the initial stages you should give your dog vegetables that can be digested easily and don't vary the menu too much, giving him a chance to get used to this new 'firework of tastes'. Please bear in mind that you don't have to offer balanced meals on a daily basis. It is much more important that the diet is balanced over a longer period of time.

At the beginning you should avoid feeding bones to your dog, because their digestive system has to get used to the fresh food diet first. In order to make sure they get enough calcium you can either feed dried eggshells or calcium citrate.

My everyday tip
Crush the dried eggshells with a pestle and mortar. If you still own an old coffee grinder for decorative purposes, you should breathe new life into it. This device is perfect for grinding eggshells. Make sure the old coffee has been removed and the grinder cleaned thoroughly first!

Dried dog food and fresh foods are digested in different ways. Make sure there is a gap of twelve hours when switching diets.

It is possible that the dog's 'winds' will become a little more intensive in the changeover phase. You'll just have to live through that. Once the dog has got used to the fresh food diet, they usually disappear completely. If the smell is bothering you, mix a little ground caraway seed into the food. Fennel and aniseed also support the digestive process. In addition the dog's breath will also smell more neutral.

*In order to calculate the required daily amount
you need to know how much the dog weighs.*

The right proportions

It is usually said that a dog's daily food requirement is about two to three percent of their body weight. The following guideline can be applied – according to this calculation a dog weighing ten kilograms should get 200 to 300 grams, a dog weighing 40 kilograms should get 800 to 1,200 grams.

Of course this also depends on the type of dog. If he is an energetic runner, or a hectic little tyke, he will certainly need more than a dog who spends the majority of the day asleep in his basket. You'll notice very quickly whether your dog needs more or less food, because you can spot any physical change very quickly in a dog who is on a raw meat diet. Don't worry; after a very short time you will have worked out the proportional amounts that are right for your dog perfectly. Although the kitchen scales are indispensible at the beginning, you will soon be able to manage to get the correct amounts by rule of thumb.

The recommended proportions of meat and vegetables can vary. For example depending on who you ask the recommended amount of meat ranges from 30 to 70 percent, with the remainder consisting of fruit and vegetables. The dog's power output, age, growth and health status also have to be taken into account for this. A lactating bitch or a busy working dog will have different needs from those of a family dog who is not particularly active. In due course every dog owner will be able to determine the proportions of meat, fruit and vegetables that are best for his or her charge.

According to the proportions of meat and vegetables that I apply myself, a dog weighing ten kilograms is fed with about 130 to 200 grams of vegetables and with 70 to 100 grams of meat daily. Accordingly a dog weighing 40 kilograms would get 530 to 800 grams vegetables and 270 to 400 grams meat. The proportions of meat and vegetables for older dogs can be adjusted to fifty–fifty. After a while you develop a sixth sense as far as the appropriate amounts are concerned, because it also

The dog gets two parts of vegetables to one part of meat in their bowl.

depends on what the dog gets up to on a particular day. For instance, my very active ten kilo terrier gets 200 grams of meat and 400 grams of vegetables. This is how different individual dogs can be! Just make a start following these recommendations, and gradually adapt the individual rations to the specific needs of your dog.

My everyday tip

If your dog is a bit overweight, simply increase the proportion of vegetables. You will see the pounds falling away without your dog having to go hungry.

Where to source fresh meat?

Many larger towns have shops that offer fresh pet food. Have a look at your local business directory under pet food, foodstuffs, pet shop. It might be a good idea to ring the pet shop and enquire whether they have fresh or frozen meat in stock prior to venturing out. Not every retailer keeps their deep-freeze well stocked at all times. Make absolutely sure you check the best-before date!

You can also order fresh meat on the internet. The quality of the meat from internet retailers is generally satisfactory to very good. However, delivery times and conditions can vary substantially. Once you have chosen a particular internet retailer and are ready to order, it would be advisable to ring the customer hotline to ask about their delivery times. The online shops deliver using the postal service or a courier. Because the meat should be kept cold with as few interruptions as possible, it is important that you are at home, or ask a reliable neighbour to take in the delivery and put it in the fridge straightaway. You may encounter supply problems in the summer, because some shops don't deliver fresh meat above certain temperatures. In this case it is often possible to get frozen foods from the same retailer instead.

You could also ask a butcher whom you trust whether it might be possible to get some offal. Ignore the negative connotations of the word.

Phone first: not all pet food stores have fresh or frozen meat in stock.

Game can be fed to dogs. Contact the hunting authority in your area.

The offal is derived from animals that are designated for human consumption. At times of reduced demand the butcher will probably be very happy to sell you any leftovers at a good price.

If there is a hunter among your circle of friends, invest in this friendship! Game is a delicacy, for dogs as much as it is for humans. Let your friend know that you are interested in game, and he will be very likely to remember you next time he's had a hunting success. However, since demand for game is very high, he will probably prefer to reserve the meat for your personal consumption. More appropriate as dog-meat are animals that have been killed in an accident, because these animals are no longer suitable for human consumption. Game means that the animal, for example deer or hare, has not been kept in an enclosure, but has been raised in its natural habitat with a lot of running space and with the best foods the environment can offer. The allegation that dogs who are fed on game will go hunting in the forest is a persistent rumour and is, of course, not true! However, wild boar should not appear on the dog's menu, because of the risk of catching the Aujesky's disease virus (see 'Meat – which type is suitable?').

If you encounter a small gap in supply you can simply buy the meat from the nearest supermarket. Again, keep a keen eye on the best-before date. Because usually you have no way of knowing how long the meat has been lying on the counter, you should either serve it in the bowl immediately or freeze it straight away.

However, the supermarket option should remain the exception when sourcing meat. In contrast to the 'dog-meat butcher' or the internet, supermarket meat is disproportionately expensive. In addition, if more dogs are fed meat that has been reared for human consumption, more meat has to be reared and produced. But because in a butcher's shop there will always be high quality leftovers which would otherwise be thrown away, it makes sense to source the meat for your dog from there.

Make it a rule to buy the meat in large chunks. Once meat has been cut into small pieces, or moreover, if it has been minced, it keeps for a much shorter time. While you can store larger pieces in the fridge for two or three days, minced meat has to be fed or frozen immediately.

My everyday tip
Go and visit your local abattoir. You will probably enter into a conversation. You may meet the person from whom you can source your dog meat for the next few years. Don't be afraid of this visit. The butcher's section will be open to the public.

The ingredients

Meat - which type is suitable?

Generally the beef on offer in pet food stores is pure muscle meat, meat from the mouth, rumen, omasum, heart, gullet, liver and mixed meats.

Sometimes you will also find meat from poultry. Also suitable are lamb and horse meat. Generally any kind of meat can be used as dog food, including game, as already mentioned.

Pork (wild or domestic) should be avoided as a matter of course. Pigs can pass the deadly Aujeszky's disease virus on to dogs. Although in some European countries, such as Germany, pork is considered Aujeszky virus-free, it is still best to avoid it. Please bear in mind that raw pork mince is not suitable as dog food either. Innards can be on the menu once or twice a week. Rumen and omasum should be fed to the dog unwashed. If you don't wash them, you don't need to add grain flakes to the dog food, which are the principal allergy triggers.

Green, unwashed rumen and omasum contain pre-digested grains which can easily be digested by the dog. Strictly speaking heart is not an 'innard', but part of the muscle meat.

Many dogs won't eat liver raw. You need to either blanch it, or use other innards that the dog likes. Liver should be on the menu every two weeks. It provides the dog with sufficient vitamin A.

You can also offer fish to your dog. It can be fed raw and whole, or pureed. The bones can be included. They pose no risk to the dog. Fish goes off very quickly. While slightly 'off' meat can be fed to a dog without reservations, fish should be fed only when it is completely fresh. Therefore the rule is that after buying the fish, it should be fed to the dog or frozen straight away.

Keep an eye on the price of fish in your neighbourhood. Because Friday is tradition-ally the day when fish is eaten, in some regions that is when fish prices are high. On Saturdays, Mondays and Tuesdays it usually costs less.

Tinned tuna, sardines, etc. should be washed because of their high salt content. However, some dogs are so keen on fish oils that you should occasionally allow them to have some. Fish oils are also handy for making a less popular dish more palatable to the dog.

Cheek is an inexpensive meat that most dogs like.

Fish is a good source of protein. Feed it raw and whole.

Comparing prices is worthwhile: fish prices fluctuate on a daily basis.

Dogs are particularly fond of this: the smell of gullet is something of an 'acquired taste' for the human nose, however.

My everyday tip
Ask your fishmonger for belly flaps. Most are processed into fish dishes and fish cakes in the afternoon. Their price is far below the normal price of fish!

To recap – it is up to the dog owner to decide in what form or shape the meat is fed. Some dogs don't like eating large chunks of meat; others on the other hand love it. Some dogs won't eat vegetables voluntarily, making it necessary to puree meat and vegetables together.

Type of meat	Which parts	Note
Beef	You can feed any part of the meat available	Lean meat
Lamb	All parts except the gut, because it may harbour parasites	Fatty meat
Horse	Muscle, no offal	Lean meat
Poultry	You can feed any part of the meat available	Easily digestible, suitable for convalescents
Game, rabbit, hare	Everything can be fed – including the soft bones	Lean meat
Fish	The whole fish, including bones	Lean meat
Pork	Pork should never be fed	

The following calculation applies, based on the assumption that a dog should get three percent of their own body weight in food:

- Body weight in kilograms × 0.03 gives you the total amount of food in kilograms
- Body weight in kilograms × 0.01 gives you the proportion of meat in kilograms
- Body weight in kilograms × 0.02 gives you the fruit and vegetable proportion in kilograms

However, these are only guidelines. Depending on circumstances, age or daily activity, rations can be adjusted upwards or downwards. Dogs used for hunting need a larger amount of food during the hunting season. Sporty dogs who do agility training or competition dog sports should also get more food. Many dogs need larger portions in winter than they do during the warmer seasons.

Fruit and vegetables – which ones are suitable?

To enable the dog to break down, and hence absorb, the fruit and vegetables in their diet, these have to be pureed or briefly steamed. Because steaming leads to a loss of vitamins, pureeing them is actually better. Vegetables to be favoured are green vegetables such as salad leaves, courgettes or cucumbers. They contain a lot of chlorophyll, which is very valuable to the dog.

Fruit and veg play a big part in the fresh food diet.

My everyday tip
Don't discard the peelings and outer leaves when preparing vegetables and salad for the family dinner. Washed and pureed they are very suitable for canine consumption. Naturally this does not apply to leftovers that have gone off.

In principle almost any kind of vegetable can be offered. There are only very few exceptions (see chapter 'The food ingredients'; list of 'don'ts'). Dogs are generally able to digest cruciferous vegetables too, but they can cause flatulence and undesirable 'winds'. This also applies to legumes and pulses, such as peas, lentils and beans. Cruciferous vegetables become a lot more digestible for the dog once they have been steamed briefly. Members of the deadly nightshade family (solanum), such as tomatoes and peppers, contain solanin, which is toxic to carnivores. They should only be fed to the dog in a very ripe state. Aubergine, another member of the solanum family, should never be fed at all. The solanin content is just too high. Although the potato is also part of this group, it is perfectly all right to put it in the food bowl once it's been boiled.

All members of the onion family such as chives, spring onions or onions should be avoided completely. They contain sulphur compounds which in larger amounts can be harmful to dogs. Avocado does not belong in the dog's food bowl either. It contains the toxic substance persin which is poisonous for dogs. This is extremely harmful for dogs' – and also cats' – heart muscles.

Just as with vegetables, when feeding fruit you have to ensure that it is ripe. In fact it doesn't do the dog any harm, if fruit is overripe. Grapes should definitely not be given to dogs. Stone fruit have to have to be de-stoned because the stones are harmful to the dog.

Because of cost considerations and also from an ecological point of view, fruit and vegetables should be selected according to their seasonal availability.

My everyday tip
Wash potatoes before peeling them for the family meal, and briefly boil the peelings until they are soft. The boiled peelings contain lots of vitamins and are easily digestible for the dog.

x – available from retailers at low prices

x – from local fields

	Jan	Feb	March	April	May	June	July	Aug	Sep	Oct	Nov	Dec
Apple	X	X	X	X	X	X	X	X	X	X	X	X
Apricots					X	X	X	X	X			
Asparagus****		X	X	X	X	X						
Banana¹	X	X	X	X	X	X	X	X	X	X	X	X
Blackberries							X	X	X	X		
Blueberries						X	X	X	X			
Brussel sprouts***	X	X	X	X	X				X	X	X	X
Carrots	X	X	X	X	X	X	X	X	X	X	X	X
Cauliflower***	X	X	X	X	X	X	X	X	X	X	X	X
Celeriac	X	X	X						X	X	X	X
Cherries	X	X	X	X	X	X	X	X	X			
Chicory	X	X	X	X					X	X	X	X
Courgettes	X	X	X	X	X	X	X				X	X
Cranberries						X	X	X	X	X	X	
Cress*	X	X	X	X	X	X	X	X	X	X	X	X
Cucumber	X	X	X	X	X	X	X	X	X	X	X	X
Currants						X	X	X	X			
Fennel	X	X	X	X	X	X	X	X	X	X	X	X
Herbs*	X	X	X	X	X	X	X	X	X	X	X	X
Kiwifruit¹	X	X	X	X	X	X	X	X	X	X	X	X
Kohlrabi***	X	X	X	X	X	X	X	X	X	X		
Leafy salads	X	X	X	X	X	X	X	X	X	X	X	X
Nectarines¹						X	X	X	X			
Oranges¹	X	X	X	X	X	X					X	X
Peaches						X	X	X	X			
Pears	X	X	X	X	X	X	X	X	X	X	X	X
Pineapple¹	X	X	X	X	X	X	X	X	X	X	X	X
Plums						X	X	X	X	X		
Potatoes**	X	X	X	X	X	X	X	X	X	X	X	X
Pumpkin							X	X	X	X	X	X
Raspberries						X	X	X	X			
Savoy cabbage***	X	X	X	X	X	X	X	X	X	X	X	X
Strawberries			X	X	X	X	X	X				
Turnips	X	X	X	X	X	X	X	X	X	X	X	X

¹ not grown in this county, has to be imported

* grown in your own garden or frozen

** feed only once boiled

*** is one of the cruciferous vegetables that cause flatulence and should therefore be lightly steamed

**** only feed in small amounts

The 'don'ts' list at a glance

Avocado	Some types contain the toxin persin; can be lethal for dogs.	Never feed these!
Chocolate/cocoa	The alkaloid has a negative effect on the dog's cardiovascular system, can be lethal.	Don't ever leave chocolate lying around where the dog can find it.
Cruciferous vegetables: Cauliflower, Brussels sprouts, broccoli, kohlrabi, greens	Hard to digest; can cause flatulence and tummy cramps.	The various types of cruciferous vegetables are generally well tolerated when boiled, and can be added to the diet.
Grapes	May cause kidney damage.	Never feed these! Raisins too are unsuitable for dogs.
Legumes and pulses: Peas, lentils, beans	Hard to digest; may cause flatulence and tummy cramps.	Legumes and pulses can be fed in small amounts after cooking.
Onion plants: Chives, leeks, spring onions, shallots, garlic	Contain solanin; not suitable for dogs.	Never feed these! There is, however a debate regarding whether garlic is unsuitable for dogs. In small amounts it is supposed to be effective against fleas.
Solanum family: Tomatoes, aubergines, peppers, pepperoni, except potatoes	Contain the toxin solanin when unripe.	Tomatoes and peppers can be fed if they are very ripe and in small amounts. Always avoid aubergines. Boiled potatoes can be offered without reservation.
Stones from stone fruit	Fruit stones contain deadly cyanide.	In the garden too, keep a watchful eye on your dog and prevent them from eating stone fruit.

It has to be said, however, that the toxicity sometimes lies in the quantity. If you are of the opinion – and many dog owners are – that garlic offers protection against fleas and ticks, you can feed a little garlic segment or a little garlic powder without worry.

Many cereal flake mixtures contain leeks. In small quantities leek is also not harmful to the dog. Leek is mixed in with the flakes because dogs like the taste, and because the food mixture smells more appetising to the dog owner which will entice them to buy it again.

Not everything the dog may like is safe. Grapes are also taboo.

At this point I'd like to reiterate that the feeding of additional expensive cereal mixtures is not necessary.

And if the dog helps himself to the odd apple with pips at harvest time, that shouldn't make him sick either!

Milk and dairy products

Milk and dairy products are nutritionally irrelevant to the dog's diet. Many dogs can't even tolerate them and get bad indigestion. However, there are also dogs who consider cream or cottage cheese, quark or yoghurt a delicacy. If your dog likes these products and is able to digest them well, there is no reason why you should not to mix a spoonful in with their food every now and again. Cream is an appropriate foodstuff to help fatten up an emaciated dog. And licking clean a yoghurt tub is great fun for a dog. If they don't get to lick yoghurt tubs too often, the amount of sugar from a fruit yoghurt is negligible.

Most dogs really like cheese. If it is used as an occasional treat during training, there is nothing wrong with that. Hard cheeses and mouldy (blue) cheeses, however, have no place in a dog's daily menu plan. In spite of all the prejudice, a dog does not lose their sense of

Dogs love licking yoghurt tubs clean.

Dogs should always have access to fresh water; milk is no alternative.

smell after enjoying a piece of cheese. The reason why a dog should only get small amounts of cheese is the high salt content.

My everyday tip

If you're offering a meal to your dog that consists of something unfamiliar to him, and he doesn't like it, you can sprinkle a little grated Parmesan cheese over the food. He will in all likelihood eat it then. Of course you shouldn't make a habit of this.

To substitute water with milk is completely unacceptable! There should always be enough fresh water available for the dog to drink. You will notice, however, that the dog will drink quite a lot less on the fresh food diet than during periods of eating dried or tinned food, because the fresh food contains far more moisture. However, a freshly filled water bowl is always vital for a dog.

The bone ration

Bones are an important component of the fresh food diet. They must never be fed boiled, fried or grilled. Once warmed up, bones can splinter and hurt the dog internally. Also, raw long bones from chicken or turkey for example (wings and legs) should never be given to a dog, because of the risk of splintering. All other raw bones, on the other hand, will provide your dog with calcium, enzymes, fat, proteins and minerals. In addition the dog will be kept occupied with their meal for quite a long time. A dog who is able to digest bones well will look forward to their bone ration as if it were a banquet.

You should only introduce bones to the dog's diet once their digestive system has adjusted to the fresh food diet. Prior to this you have to keep an eye on their calcium intake. Ground eggshells added to the dog food contain a lot of calcium. Bananas, seaweed, parsley, spinach and cress also contain valuable calcium. A fully grown healthy dog needs 50 milligrams of calcium per kilogram of body weight. According to this, a dog weighing 10 kilograms will need five grams of bone or a third of a teaspoon of eggshells daily, or you can give them a supplement from the pharmacy. Surplus calcium represents no risk to an adult dog. They will excrete it. However, you should keep an eye on the amount of calcium given to puppies and young dogs during the growth phase. Because there would be no point in giving a tiny portion of bone to the dog every day, it makes sense to concentrate on one or two servings of bone per week. To re-cap: a dog does not need every single component of a healthy diet every day. However, over a longer period of time the dog should be fed a balance of minerals, vitamins, calcium, etc.

Bones are a real highlight for a dog.

Calcium is a very important nutritional component, for dogs as well as humans.

Bananas

Seaweed

Eggshell

Spinach

Parsley

Celeriac

Watercress

Calcium provider

Turkey necks are great for beginners.

Crushed eggshells can be a substitute for the bone ration.

To get the dog used to eating bone, at the beginning it is advisable to go for cartilage and soft bones that are easy to chew for the dog. Raw chicken and turkey necks or beef gullet are very well suited for this purpose. Please bear in mind; cartilage is not bone and does not contain particularly large amounts of calcium.

Soft veal bones are also suitable for a beginner. Later on marrow bones, slices of beef leg bone, or ox tails provide a challenge for the dog.

Some dogs react to eating bone by producing whitish crumbly stools that the dog finds hard to pass. These hard 'deposits' are called bone stool. You can avoid bone stools by feeding bones with a lot of meat on them. If your dog has a tendency to have problems in that department, you should stop feeding them bone, and fall back on eggshells and supplements, in order to ensure their calcium intake.

If your dog tends to produce bone stools, please stop giving them bones altogether. Don't force them to eat bones because you are of the opinion that bones ought to be part of the fresh food diet. Again and again there are cases of dogs at veterinary clinics who need to be given enemas or even an operation in order to remove bone stool.

Which types of bone are suitable?
• Beef: All cartilage such as the gullet, windpipe, throat, but also marrow bones,

slices of leg, breast, ribs, ox tail, spine, shoulder.

- Lamb: Marrow bones, slices of leg, gullet, ribs, spine.
- Poultry: Necks, ribs, spine, chicken trimmings.
- Game, rabbit, hare: All soft bones can be used as food.
- Pork: Should be avoided completely!

Grain

Grain is surplus to a dog's optimum dietary requirements. The dog's digestive system is not able to make use of grain at all. Some dog owners feed grain as a stomach filler. If you are feeding grain, you should bear in mind that the grain has to be either boiled or at least soaked, before putting it in the dog's food bowl.

Rice with chicken is the preferred food in cases of diarrhoea.

Many animals develop grain allergies. This is one of the reasons why people switch from ready-made food to feeding fresh foods. Some dried foods in particular have an extremely high grain content. This doesn't make them particularly useful in terms of a dog's dietary requirements.

If the dog can tolerate grain and does not get an allergic reaction, there is no reason why you couldn't give them an old bread roll or some pasta left over from a family meal.

As a bland convalescent diet, after diarrhoea attacks or other illnesses, the feeding of rice and chicken or fish is often recommended. Although rice is a grain, it can be fed to dogs, if they can digest it well. However, it has to be boiled extensively to enable the dog's digestive system to break it down. Also bear in mind that rice is a strong diuretic, meaning that a dog fed on rice will have to urinate more frequently. Over a longer period of time rice cannot be used as a substitute for vegetables.

Nutritional supplements

Besides the main components, meat and vegetables, the feeding of nutritional supplements is required, or recommended. This includes oils and herbs for example, but also nuts and other supplements. Oils are very important for the fresh food diet, because some vegetables, such as carrots, cannot be absorbed without oils. Herbs and supplements such as healing earth or linseed gruel can be used to alleviate minor complaints.

My everyday tip
Try the new oils on your salad one of these days. You will be surprised how tasty and highly digestible they are. However, I don't recommend salmon oil because of the smell!

Some vegetables such as carrots can only be absorbed in conjunction with oils.

Because the dog absorbs a large quantity of omega-6 oils as part of the fresh food diet, oils with high omega-3 fatty acid content have to be supplemented. These two fatty acids are in fact antagonists and have to be present in a balanced ratio to each other. Therefore the oils you add to the dog's meals should have high omega-3 fatty acid content. These include walnut oil, rapeseed oil, flax oil, linseed oil, fish oil and hemp oil. Cod-liver oil has also contains large quantities of omega-3 fatty acids. It should not be given to the dog too often, however.

My everyday tip

Fish oils, salmon oil for instance, have quite a strong smell, and are therefore loved by dogs. They are therefore very useful for mixing in with foods that the dog is not particularly fond of.

Salt and oils

Contrary to the commonly held belief that dogs should not have any salt, the 'white gold' is actually a dietary requirement, unless you have the opportunity to mix some fresh blood into the dog's food. Blood contains a lot of salt. In households where this is not an option, a pinch of untreated sea salt can be added to the dog's food twice a week. If you reward your dog with a piece of cheese or sausage as an occasional treat, you can omit the extra pinch of salt, because both products contain salt.

Oils should be given to the dog at least three to four times a week. The respective quantities are subject to a number of factors. Should your canine friend need to lose some weight, just use a little less oil than you would for a dog with a trim figure.

You can alleviate skin and coat problems by adding extra oil. Very active dogs can also be given oils on a daily basis. Alternating between the different oils provides variation in the diet and in the dosage of the essential fatty acids. Dogs who are mostly fed game don't need as many omega-3 fatty acids, because the meat of wild animals does not contain as many omega-6 fatty acids, making it unnecessary to offset a surplus with omega-3 fatty acids. When dealing with minor health issues additional types of oil might also come in handy.

Oils

Black cumin oil	Is effective for respiratory complaints and has a positive influence on milk production in lactating bitches.
Coconut oil, shavings	Used for worm prevention.
Evening primrose oil	Helpful for skin problems, has anti-inflammatory qualities; can be given to diabetes sufferers as well.
Fish oil	Rich in omega-3 fatty acids.
Flax oil	Rich in omega-3 fatty acids, can offer protection from bone and joint disease.
Hemp oil	Rich in omega-3 fatty acids, strengthens the immune system and used topically it helps with healing small wounds.
Linseed oil	Rich in omega-3 fatty acids; improves coat condition and can assist in dealing with inflammation.
Pumpkin oil	In male dogs it is used for prostate conditions, in females for nervous bladder complaints.
Rapeseed oil	Rich in omega-3 fatty acids; can lower blood cholesterol levels and has a positive effect on the immune system.
Safflower oil	Very helpful as a compress for sprains and contusions.
Walnut oil	Rich in omega-3 fatty acids, improves the fluidity of the blood and strengthens the immune system; rich in vitamins.

Further supplementary foods

Various different herbs and seeds should also be added to the dog's menu plan. They contain a lot of vitamins and minerals. You can also use herbs to treat some minor health problems. This is how it's done: in order to enable the dog to break them down, the herbs have to be made into a puree or given as

Coconut shavings should be a regular part of the menu, because they help with worm prevention.

a powder. The good thing about herbs is that you can grow them yourself, and they are available all year round. If you dry the harvested herbs, they can be preserved for a long time. Or you can freeze them in the ice cube tray with some added water. This way they can easily be made into handy portions. Deep-frozen herbs from the supermarket are also suitable. Herbs should not be fed to the dog in large amounts and not on a daily basis. Caution: you should avoid giving large amounts of herbs to pregnant bitches. Many herbs can cause a miscarriage or premature birth. You should also be very careful with regard to dogs suffering from epilepsy.

Coconut shavings play a great part in the raw food diet. Scattered over the dog food every day or several times a week they work as a worm prophylaxis. The same goes for coconut fat and coconut oil. For an overweight dog less generous amounts of oil would be advisable. Adding coconut oil to the dog's diet is not a substitute for stool examinations carried out by the vet. For this you should

Aloe vera	Has detox and anti-inflammatory effects, can be used topically for insect bites and small inflammations. Ask your pharmacist for an edible aloe vera gel.
Apple vinegar	Stimulates the metabolism and helps against flatulence and constipation.
Basil	Helps against stress, exhaustion and nervous conditions, used topically it has antibacterial properties. Don't feed to pregnant bitches!
Caraway seeds	Crushed and made into a gruel, they soothe and calm the gastrointestinal tract.
Coconut	Is used for worm prevention, but does have a lot of calories.
Dandelion	Helps against itching and detoxifies the liver.
Egg and eggshell	An egg per week makes the coat shiny, crushed eggshells are a substitute for bone ration.
Fennel seeds	Crushed and made into a gruel, they are very useful for indigestion; one teaspoon per meal is enough.
Green-lipped mussel extract	Good for coat and skin; supports the digestive system if there is excess stomach acid.
Healing earth	Used as prophylaxis and to ameliorate joint and connective tissue complaints.
Linseed	Boiled thoroughly and given before bedtime it is effective against excess stomach acid and prevents the vomiting of 'yellow slime'; give about one tablespoon, depending on the size of the dog.
Oregano	Has expectorant and antispasmodic effects; used for coughs.
Parsley	Has an activating effect on tired dogs, diuretic, vitamin rich.
Peppermint	Supportive for gastrointestinal complaints, kills germs, fights pain.
Raspberry leaves	Active against diarrhoea, cleanses and fights pain.
Sage	Has a calming effect during anxiety attacks; against colds, coughs and inflammation of the lining of the gut; is supposed to help against worms.
Stinging nettle	Helps prevent rheumatism and arthritis; diuretic effect.
Thyme	A great remedy for asthma and coughs; has strong expectorant properties.

provide three samples from three different dog-walking expeditions, because worms are not necessarily present in every 'little pile'.

> **My everyday tip**
> If you want to collect the herbs yourself, make sure you avoid picking any leaves growing close to roads and industrial plants. These herbs will be badly contaminated.

Pepping up ready-made food

Those who are still a little hesitant about changing over to feeding fresh meat can improve the quality of ready-made food with added extras. You can for instance mix a spoonful of cottage cheese into the wet food, or offer the dried food with a little added oil or an egg.

> **My everyday tip**
> For those of you who have a garden, you can always give the egg whole. This way the dog will have to 'unwrap' the treat himself, which doubles the enjoyment. Eggs can be offered boiled as well as raw.

As far as feeding the dog is concerned, enjoyment and fun should be a major aspect for both – the dog as well as the human! Once you start pepping up the ready-made food, you will quickly acquire a 'taste' for it and you'll want to know more about a species-appropriate diet. Many fresh food feeders have come to the raw food diet via this path.

The menu plan

The basic shopping list

Before starting the fresh food diet, you have to buy those ingredients that you will need again and again in the course of the feeding routine. You should always have the following basic ingredients in the house:

• Two omega-3 fatty acid oils (e. g. linseed oil or walnut oil which have no strong taste of their own, and are usually accepted by the dog)

• Coconut shavings (one teaspoon per daily ration reduces the risk of worm infestation)

• Healing earth

My everyday tip
I use a reusable insulated bag for freezer products from the supermarket for transporting the fresh meat. This keeps the goods fresh, just in case the shopping trip takes a little longer than expected.

Shopping list for the first week

- Meat, for example beef; proportionate amounts of pure beef, one daily ration of rumen and one daily ration of omasum
- Vegetables, for example courgettes, carrots, potatoes (for boiling)
- Herbs, for example basil, parsley
- Two eggs

The weekly menu plan

What does a weekly fresh food diet menu plan look like? Which products can be fed in the transition period, and what kind of reactions may be observed in the dog as a result?

You will recall that a dog does not need the full range of minerals and vitamins every day. Personally I try to achieve a nutritionally balanced diet for my dog over a four-week period.

Fresh vegetables are the basis of a healthy diet for dogs – but avoid the onion!

An example for the adjustment week

During the adjustment week the feeding of bone is completely omitted. Calcium is fed in the form of eggshell or via a supplement from the pharmacy. Your dog's digestive tract has to adjust to the new diet first. Feed those

Inexpensive and easily digestible: beef is a main component of the fresh meat diet.

If you puree meat and veg together, your dog can't pick out the lumps of meat.

vegetables that you assume your dog will be able to tolerate. You have to decide for yourself and your dog whether you want to feed one, two or several meals per day. If you feed several rations, simply divide the amount for the whole day into individual portions accordingly. If your dog does not like the raw meat at first, you can blanch it. If they reject the vegetables, simply puree the meat together with the vegetables.

If you occasionally give your dog a piece of cheese or sausage, this will provide enough salt in the diet, and no extra dose is required. If they don't get these in-between treats, a small pinch of salt twice a week will suffice.

You should observe your dog closely during the adjustment phase. In order to allow the dog to get used to the new diet, you should not feed too many different components. You will notice that their digestion times will be

Monday	Pure beef, boiled potatoes, a teaspoon of coconut shavings, walnut oil, possibly a pinch of salt
Tuesday	Beef rumen, boiled potatoes, courgettes, a teaspoon of coconut shavings, an egg – the eggshell is dried, crushed and mixed into the food
Wednesday	Pure beef, boiled potatoes, carrots, a teaspoon of coconut shavings, walnut oil
Thursday	Pure beef, courgettes, carrots, linseed oil, a teaspoon of coconut shavings, possibly a pinch of salt
Friday	Pure beef, boiled potatoes, walnut oil, one egg with eggshell
Saturday	Omasum, apple, courgette, a teaspoon of coconut shavings
Sunday	Beef, boiled potatoes, carrots, linseed oil

somewhat prolonged. In the first few days, processing the fresh foods takes the dog's digestive system a little more effort than ready-made food. It will be trained up in due course and the digestion period will get shorter again. You have to decide for how long you want to stick to the adjustment menu plan. This adjustment menu plan contains all the vitamins and minerals a dog requires. Even if the adjustment phase takes a little longer, there is no risk of malnutrition.

It is also possible to combine fresh foods with the dog's familiar food during the adjustment phase. You can feed the familiar food in the morning and the new, fresh food in the evening. Fresh food and dried food are processed differently by the dog, and the time it takes to digest them can vary considerably. Therefore it is necessary to allow an interval of twelve hours between feeding dried food and fresh food, in order to avoid stressing the dog's digestive system. With tinned food the interval is of less significance.

After the adjustment phase

After the adjustment phase you can begin to introduce a 'bone ration'. Good bones for beginners are, for instance, cartilage such as beef throat, raw chicken and turkey necks, or ox tail pieces. Particularly at the beginning the bone should be fed with a lot of meat, in order to prevent hard 'bone' stools. Leg slices or meaty bones are particularly useful for this.

Please bear in mind that the proportion of calcium in cartilage is not particularly high, making it necessary to add eggshell or a supplement from the pharmacy. If the dog has no previous experience with gnawing bone,

In a diagram the adjustment phase looks like this:

	Mon	Tue	Wed	Thur	Fri	Sat	Sun
Coconut	x	x	x	x		x	
Egg/eggshell		x			x		
Innards		x				x	
Meat	x		x	x	x		x
Oil	x		x	x	x		x
Possibly salt	x			x			
Vegetables	x	x	x	x	x	x	x

*Leg slices provide the perfect meal:
a lot of meat with bone.*

they should not be left unsupervised at the beginning. They will learn quickly, however.

Many dogs have little idea what to do with their first bone. They'll carry it around the house looking for a place to hide it. In order to avoid this – and the resulting cleaning – you can assign a special place, a machine-washable blanket in the kitchen for instance, as the permanent spot for eating bone.

The first few times your dog may try to carry the bone off somewhere else. Loving insistence will teach them in a relatively short period of time that they are only allowed to chew the bones in this particular spot.

What's that? OK, you've talked me into it – I'll take it!

This dog is waiting eagerly for his bone.

My everyday tip

Put an offcut of a Teflon-coated material on top of the blanket on which your dog eats their bones. Teflon can be wiped clean as well as washed. This way you don't have to put the blanket in the washing machine after each use.

Even if your dog is a bit sceptical when it comes to their first bone, don't take away the bone, but leave it on the blanket. In most cases the dog will come back to check on it a couple of times, and then happily eat it. Once your dog has been 'converted' to eating their bone ration, they should only get one egg per week. After the introduction of the 'bone ration' dogs who are only fed once a day don't get vegetables one day per week. This does not cause a nutritional shortfall, because it is the sum of meals fed over a longer period of time that matters. Dogs who are enjoying two meals per day can get a vegetable ration in the morning and a bone ration in the evening. I prepare the dog's meals for one whole day in the afternoon. I keep back one third for the next morning. This means that I don't have to clean the blender twice a day.

Monday	In the morning: Bone ration In the evening: Meat, vegetables, coconut shavings, oil, possibly salt
Tuesday	In the morning: Last night's leftovers In the evening: Innards, vegetables, coconut shavings
Wednesday	In the morning: Last night's leftovers In the evening: Meat, vegetables, coconut shavings, egg
Thursday	In the morning: Last night's leftovers In the evening: Meat, vegetables, oil, coconut shavings, possibly salt
Friday	In the morning: Last night's leftovers In the evening: Bone ration
Saturday	In the morning: Cartilage (chicken neck, windpipe) In the evening: Innards, vegetables, coconut shavings
Sunday	In the morning: Last night's leftovers In the evening: Fish, vegetables, oil

In a diagram:

	Mon	Tue	Wed	Thur	Fri	Sat	Sun
Bone	x				x		
Cartilage						x	
Coconut	x	x	x	x	x	x	x
Egg			x	x			
Fish							x
Innards		x	x	x		x	x
Meat	x	x		x	x		
Oil	x	x		x	x		x
Possibly salt	x	x			x		
Vegetables	x	x	x	x	x	x	x

You can see from this example how balanced the dog's diet can look over the period of one week. The fact that there are some days when meat and innards are both on the menu is the result of feeding part of the evening ration the following morning. Here a meat ration was substituted by a fish ration. Many dog owners have their dogs fast on one day of the week. This does not do the dog any harm. And if your dog has an excess few grams on their frame, it may even be a good idea. The fast day should be on a day when the dog is due to get pure meat, in order to avoid them skipping the innards. Fast days are not absolutely necessary. Dogs that are particularly active should be fed every day of the week.

An alternative to the fast day can be a meat-less day. If your dog is able to tolerate milk products, on vegetarian days the pureed vegetables can be refined with a bit of cottage cheese or yoghurt. Whether you decide to have a fast day or a vegetarian day is up to you. However, the meat-free day each week should be kept to, in order to allow the dog's kidneys a day off.

Active dogs can have a vegetarian day instead of a fast day – it gives the kidneys some respite.

The fresh food diet on holiday

Short holidays in your own country normally present no problem at all. The meat can be transported in a cool box which will preserve it for three to four days. Even if the meat is a little 'off', it can be fed to the dog without reservation. The vegetables can be bought and processed fresh locally (remember not to forget the hand blender or the grater!) or they can be frozen and stored in the cool box. You could also feed baby food from little jars. This solution is a little more pricey, however. You will need to take the oils and supplements with you from home.

My everyday tip
Collect some empty screw-lid jars (caper or pesto jars, for example). When you're on holiday they can be used to transport oils and other additional foods. This means you don't have to take any large packages with you.

The fresh food diet on holiday is not as complicated as you might think.

When on holiday, the meat should be transported in as large chunks as possible. Once meat is cut up into small pieces it goes off a lot quicker.

Trips abroad make carrying fresh meat a little more complicated. Due to certain unforeseeable events, the rules and regulations for importing foodstuffs can change very rapidly (for example because of outbreaks of foot and mouth disease, bird flu or something similar). Therefore you have to find out about any import restrictions that may apply to the individual countries before starting on your journey. This kind of information is available from embassies, consulates or tourist boards. If there is an import ban, it is best to buy fresh produce locally.

I'm admittedly a little lazy when I'm on holiday. I bring back sufficient amounts of potatoes and carrots, then boil and mash the potatoes as well as the carrots, and put the large bowl with the mash in the fridge. Then I take the daily ration for the dog, add fresh beef mince and a dash of oil – and it's ready.

Some days I get some bones for the dog which I buy locally. Because our holidays usually last a maximum of three weeks, malnutrition will not be a problem, if I make sure that I feed the dog a very varied diet once we're back home, or even put him on a special

Beef mince from the supermarket is a very handy food while on holiday.

expect this problem to sort itself out after a few days. You should of course choose a good quality food for the 'holiday food'.

If you use dried food, make sure that the proportion of grain is not too high. Interested dog owners will be able to get good advice from their specialist retailer.

There are tinned foods that contain 100 percent cooked meat. Read the information on the tin very carefully. If it says that the contents of the tin are not suitable to be fed as a sole food, you have to add vegetables and oils. In my view this is a good alternative for the most enjoyable time of the year. If the tinned food has been declared to be a sole food, the meat contains added ingredients. It is definitely not pure meat.

spring diet for a week (see 'Treating everyday complaints').

A healthy dog can also be fed on tinned and dried food during the holiday period. This is no problem at all. However, you should check beforehand whether your dog actually likes this food. Having said that, no dog has ever been known to have starved in front of a well-filled food bowl, therefore one would

My everyday tip

You can find out from the manufacturer whether it might be possible to get the ready-made food locally. This saves having to carry tins or sacks of dog food all the way to your holiday destination.

Fresh food diet for puppies and older dogs

Of course puppies and older dogs can also be fed on a fresh meat diet. This is pretty simple and straightforward. Depending on their age a puppy gets three to four portions a day, that's four to five percent of their body weight per day. Because a little puppy is growing all the time, they ought to be weighed – depending on the adult size of the breed – at least once, preferably three times, a week. In the first months of a puppy's life you should omit meals consisting of pure bone, especially hard bones. Chicken necks and windpipes for example consist of cartilage, which even a puppy should be able to cope with. If at the beginning you

Nothing could be fresher than this: Saluki offspring at the puppy bar.

want to avoid bones and cartilage altogether, you will have to add the calcium some other way. You can also put a whole chicken with bones through the meat grinder and feed portions of that to the puppy instead. For a dog breeder it would make sense to get a good, strong meat grinder as an additional piece of equipment. There is no need to do this if you are able to find a nearby butcher who will kindly mince whole chickens for you.

It is important to bear in mind that growing puppies have a greater calcium requirement than adult dogs. For puppies who are fed on four meals per day, two meals can be made up of chicken necks or minced chicken, and the other two can consist of meat with vegetables and oil. As a general rule you can feed portions of one-third meat with two-thirds vegetables.

Older dogs (large breeds from the age of eight, smaller breeds form the age of ten) also need different things from the food they get in their bowls every day. This starts with the proportions of vegetables and meat. Older dogs need to derive even more highly digestible proteins from the meat content of their diet. For oldies you therefore have to increase the proportion of meat to at least 50 percent. Because many older dogs have problems with their figure, you should feed easily digestible meats to stouter animals. This includes all white meat, fish and very lean meat.

Of course if your oldie is of a breed that tends to get emaciated in old age, you have to increase the amount of meat accordingly, and

Chicken is easily digestible and has few calories.

Eggshells need to be fed when a dog no longer eats bones.

feed meat with more fat. As your dog gets older it becomes particularly important to keep an eye on your best friend's figure. An overweight dog will tend to have more problems with ageing joints than a dog with a trim figure.

Some older dogs are no longer able to cope with bones, or maybe only with very soft ones. In this case you have to substitute them with crushed eggshells or calcium citrate.

If an old dog can't or doesn't want to eat bones any more, you have to pay extra attention to their dental care. This means that you either need to clean the dog's teeth, or you have to get the tartar removed by a vet on a regular basis.

Old dogs often have the same problem as humans: they don't drink enough fluids during the course of the day. This can cause kidney problems.

My everyday tip
If your dog drinks conspicuously little, simply prepare their food with a little extra water. This way you can ensure that your dog takes enough fluids.

Generally it can be observed, however, that dogs who are fed on a fresh food diet tend to drink less, because the food does not swell up in the stomach, which increases the need for water. Smaller 'oldie-problems' such as a lacklustre coat or dandruff can be addressed by adding natural ingredients.

Treating everyday complaints

Curing minor ailments through diet

It is possible to use dietary measures for therapeutic purposes. Naturally in the case of illness a visit to the vet is mandatory. However, minor ailments and complaints can be alleviated by feeding various foods and nutritional supplements, or these can act in support of any veterinary treatment. If you're using dietary measures to support the therapeutic effects of a certain medication, you should always discuss this with the vet first, in order to avoid complications. You should also seek expert advice if you're feeling unsure. Premature self-diagnosis and treatments can slow the healing process considerably and have dire consequences.

The ailments and helpful herbs

Anxiety, stress	Sage, basil
Arthritis, joint and connective tissue weaknesses	Stinging nettle, green-lipped mussel extract, ginger, quark***, algae, apple vinegar
Bad breath	Parsley, fennel
Birthing cramps	Raspberry leaves (prophylactic)
Chronic pain	Ginger
Colds	Sage, linden blossom*, elderflower*, camomile*, fennel, ginger
Conjunctivitis, eye discharge	Eyebright (as drops), boiled milk (for cleansing)
Constipation	Yoghurt, cottage cheese, apple vinegar
Cough	Thyme, ribwort leaves, sage, oregano, honey, fennel
Dermatitis	Evening primrose oil, honey, calendula**
Diarrhoea	Blackberry leaves, raspberry leaves, grated apple, brown healing earth, ginger
Disinfection	Basil (topical), calendula (topical), tea tree oil (topical)
Fatigue	Parsley, sage
Flatulence	Apple vinegar, fennel, caraway seed, aniseed, healing earth
Fleas	Neem tree oil (topical), rosemary (prophylactic), coconut oil and coconut shavings (prophylactic), brown algae powder, lemon–rosemary solution (topical)
Gut bacteria, healthy	Chicory
Haematoma	Quark**, calendula**, arnica
Incontinence	Pumpkin seeds, pumpkin seed oil
Indigestion, general	Fennel seed gruel, peppermint, caraway seed gruel
Inflammation of the bladder	Bearberry leaves*, stinging nettle, parsley
Inflammation of the lining of the gut	Sage, linseed gruel
Insect bites	Onion (topical), aloe vera (topical), parsley (topical), ginger (topical)
Improving the quality of the coat	Biotin, zinc, brewer's yeast, healing earth, egg

Itching	Aloe vera (topical), dandelion (topical), ribwort (topical), balm oil (topical), watered down vinegar (topical)
Lack of appetite	Pineapple, endive salad
Labour, supporting	Raspberry leaves*, lukewarm milk
Lowering cholesterol levels	Linseed oil, sesame oil
Milk flow, supporting	Black cumin oil, dill, carrots, eggs, algae, honey, fennel seeds, alfalfa
Milk flow, suppressing	Parsley, sage
Pigmentation, loss of	Elderberry juice, elderflower
Pregnancy, supporting	Raspberry leaves, brewer's yeast, rose hip, alfalfa, seaweed
Prostate ailments	Pumpkin seeds, pumpkin seed oil
Respiratory diseases	Black cumin oil
Rheumatism	Stinging nettle
Small wounds	Hemp oil (topical), aloe vera (topical), calendula **, propolis
Sprains, contusions	Safflower oil (topical), ginger (topical)
Strengthening the immune system	Walnut oil, rapeseed oil
Teat engorgement and mastitis	Seaweed (prophylactic), camphor**, quark**, aloe vera (topical)
Travel sickness	Ginger*
Tonsillitis	Honey, sage*, warm potato peelings
Vomiting, yellow slime	Linseed gruel, brown healing earth
Worm prophylaxis	Coconut shavings, coconut oil, ginger, sage

* as a tea, mixed in with the food
** as an ointment from the pharmacy
*** as a compress, placed on the affected area

You have to be very cautious when giving herbs to pregnant bitches, possibly avoiding them altogether, because in the worst case scenario they can cause a miscarriage. This includes, for example, rosemary, sage, parsley, walnut and walnut oil.

As a rule medicinal herbs should not be fed the whole time. You get better success from a course of treatments over a period of up to three months, depending on the nature of the dog's complaints. A diarrhoea treatment should last a maximum of three days. After that, a visit to the vet cannot be avoided.

After excluding any organic problems in consultation with the vet, a course of treatment to support the dog's metabolism can be applied. The prescriptions are designed for a medium size dog weighing about thirty kilograms.

Smaller dogs get a little less, larger dogs a little more. Over- or under-dosing will not harm the dog.

Diarrhoea

Diarrhoea – apart from organic causes that have been excluded by the vet – can also be a sign of stress or excitement. The following prescription supports the dog in regaining a normal digestion.

After a food break of twenty-four hours, exclusively feed the dog on rice with blanched chicken for three days, spread out over three, or, if possible, five daily rations. Into every portion mix two tablespoons of the diarrhoea formula described as follows:

Herbs should not be fed over an extended period; a short course of treatment is much more effective.

2 tablespoons raspberry leaves
  (from the pharmacy)
2 tablespoons (Luvos) brown healing earth
  (portion bags can be obtained from the
  health food shop or pharmacy)
1 grated apple
1 pot of cottage cheese
Mix into a thick pulp with some added
carrot juice

The mixture will keep for about four days in the fridge. If the diarrhoea symptoms don't improve after three days, you will have to pay the vet another visit.

A springtime cure

After the long winter months the first rays of sun penetrate the clouds. This is a good time for human and dog to trim away the layers of winter fat and to thoroughly detox the body. The following prescription is one the dog and human can share. It should be borne in mind, however, that dandelion, parsley and stinging nettle are strong diuretics, so please plan for some extra 'walkies' with the dog. But this also helps in the fight against the winter fat!

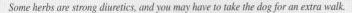

Some herbs are strong diuretics, and you may have to take the dog for an extra walk.

2 tablespoons dandelion

2 tablespoons parsley

2 tablespoons stinging nettle

1 tablespoon walnut oil

2 tablespoons cold pressed honey

Honey is a real boon for most dogs; it is tasty and healthy.

Puree the herbs with the walnut. Stir in the honey for a long time, and mix everything together to form a thick pulp. Store in the fridge. If the dog gets only a teaspoonful of the mixture with the morning and evening meals respectively, the cure will last for about eight days.

Diet for a healthy coat

The causes of a matt, lacklustre coat are varied. Taking medicines can make the dog's coat appear rough and unkempt – a side effect that can be cured with the following course of treatment. It is also recommended for the moulting period.

1 egg

½ teaspoon biotin

½ teaspoon brewer's yeast

½ teaspoon zinc

1 tablespoon salmon oil

If you give this mixture to your dog once a week over a six-week period, their coat will regenerate itself quickly and become shiny again. As a supporting measure you can also rub a mixture of mineral water and apple vinegar into the dog's coat and skin, at a ratio of ten to one. Apple vinegar works miracles with human hair too!

Cough

A cough can also be alleviated by using food-stuffs and supplements. You often hear it said that one should give the dog a child formula cough mixture. This should be avoided, unless recommended by the vet. It is debatable anyway whether cough mixtures have any effect at all.

½ tablespoon sage
1 tablespoon thyme
1 tablespoon honey
1 teaspoon fennel

Make the sage and the thyme into a tea and let it go cold. Then the honey is mixed in, the fennel crushed and also added. Offer this mixture to your dog every two days. The cough will soon loosen. If the dog won't eat this mixture on its own, you can mix it up with their food.

Chronic pain

In cases of pain you should see a vet as matter of course. It is possible, however, to speed the recovery with home remedies. The following tincture is a simple topical remedy.

1 teaspoon St John's wort
1 teaspoon ginger
1 teaspoon camomile
½ teaspoon thyme

Put all the ingredients in a pot, add half a litre of water and boil for ten minutes. Strain the herbs. Put a cloth soaked in the decoction on the painful spot and massage it in. The pain is visibly reduced.

Strengthening the immune system

3 tablespoons aloe vera gel
3 tablespoons elderberry juice
1 teaspoon rosehip powder
1 teaspoon fennel

Mix the crushed fennel seeds with the other ingredients, and put a generous tablespoonful of it into the food. This course of treatment should be given for at least six weeks. The above prescription lasts for about a week and can be stored in the fridge. In order to strengthen the immune system in the long term, lots of exercise in the fresh air is important.

Bladder weakness

Spayed bitches in particular often develop problems with a weak bladder in old age. After consulting the vet, and after a relevant treatment has been worked out and initiated, you can support the treatment by using home remedies – having discussed this with the vet.

3 tablespoons linseed oil

3 tablespoons celery juice

2 tablespoons ground pumpkin seeds

Mix the ingredients together and add 1 table-spoonful per day to the food.

Bad breath

You will notice that after changing to the fresh food diet your dog's mouth will smell much more pleasant. Tooth decay or diseases of the mucous lining in the mouth can nonetheless cause bad dog breath. Take the dog to the vet to ensure that there is no grave underlying cause. As a supporting measure you can give the dog the following mixture.

1 apple

1 carrot

1 teaspoon linseed oil

1 tablespoon cold pressed honey

Puree the ingredients in the food processor or with a hand-held blender. You can either mix the breath improver in with the food, or give it to your dog on its own. Because dogs usually love honey, it can be offered by the spoonful.

Upset stomach

Dogs often ingest something during a walk which may end up lying heavily in their stomach. As a result the dog may go off their food, become less active and feel unwell. After a food break, you can restore the dog to their former self by giving them this pulp, spread over several small meals. If the dog's condition does not improve very quickly, you will have to take them to the vet!

1 apple

1 teaspoon honey

2 carrots

1 teaspoon linseed oil

2 tablespoons camomile tea, fresh or from a tea bag

Meat stock if required

Make the camomile tea and leave it to go cold. Puree the apple and carrots with the oil, the honey and the cold camomile tea. Because dogs don't tend to consider camomile tea a culinary treat, you can add a little meat stock.

Constipation

Think back to whether your dog may have eaten too many bones. In this case the consti-pation might be the result of this. Rethink the

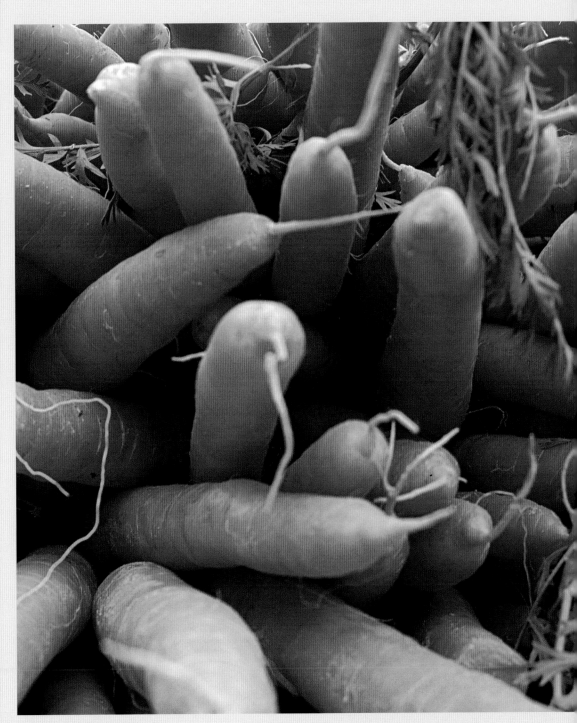

Carrots can soothe an upset tummy.

menu plan, and if necessary reduce the amount of bones.

2 slices tinned pineapple
1 apple
Grape juice
A little meat stock if required

Puree the ingredients and give the dog a tablespoon three to five times a day. If the constipation persists, of course you have to take the dog to the vet.

Apples neutralise bad smells – and not just for dogs.

Allergies

There is another reason why I am a subscribed follower of the fresh food diet. When our dog was eighteen months old, he started scratching himself very badly. After some inconclusive – and expensive – visits to the vet, following a recommendation we took the dog to Dr Vet Monika Linek's surgery. Dr Linek is a special-ist in dog dermatology, and she diagnosed our terrier with an allergy. After that we put him on an exclusion diet, and it became obvious that Yoda was allergic to the dried dog food he was given as treats. As soon as we substituted it with a different brand, the permanent scratching stopped.

Food allergies and food intolerance

A contribution by Monika Linek, Diplomate of the European College of Veterinary Dermatology

First off, it is important to understand what is actually meant by the terms 'food intolerance' and 'food allergy' respectively. Food intolerance is a non-predictable reaction to a particular food. It does not cause an immune reaction. Food allergy is an allergic or immune reaction normally to one of the protein or carbohydrate components in the diet.

Normally the protein molecules which reach the local lymphatic system of the gut via the gut barrier cause a tolerance. This means that the information is not passed on to the general immune system, but processed locally, and this is signalling to the body: 'Everything is fine, these are food components and not germs, such as for example bacteria or viruses'.

An allergic dog has a genetic predisposition not to develop this tolerance, but to react to particular food components with an exaggerated immune response. This 'overruling of tolerance' can occur at any age and as a reaction to any food component that the dog has been fed up to now. This is comparable to children who often have an allergic reaction to milk protein, wheat or nuts, or adults who suddenly develop an allergic reaction to fish, fruit or similar foods even at an advanced age.

How do you recognise a food allergy or intolerance?

Food allergies or intolerances in dogs often manifest themselves on the skin or in the gastrointestinal tract. The skin problems are variable and also non-specific. Skin-related symptoms are usually a more or less permanent general itch, licking of the paws, increased rubbing of the face and recurring ear infections. In addition, licking of the anal area, dragging and skidding on the bottom (also known as sledging) is often observed.

This is often diagnosed by the vet as a 'full anal gland', which can really only be a reaction to the irritation of the anal area, rather than the cause of the itch.

Additional symptoms often include redness, bald patches, scaly coat, an unpleasant smell, as well as pustules or scabs. These are usually secondary symptoms, because the allergic skin cannot perform the normal barrier function in defence against germs.

Dogs can also react to food intolerance and allergies by developing gastrointestinal problems. These include vomiting, diarrhoea or slimy faeces. Dog owners often report very frequent rates of defecation (more than once or twice a day).

It is estimated that 15 to 20 percent of all animals suffering food allergies with dermatological problems also have gastrointestinal symptoms, in particular frequent defecation. This seems to make sense, because frequent defecation is the result of an incomplete digestion, and food that has not been digested completely represents an increased allergy risk.

When does a food allergy or intolerance typically occur?

The symptoms can first occur at any age, although in 30 to 50 percent of cases the first signs of a food allergy occur in the first year of life. It affects all breeds, including mixed breeds. In addition the symptoms do not occur as a result of a change in feeding habits. The dog does not produce an allergic reaction to a new product, but conversely to things they have been eating for a long time, because the body has to be sensitised first.

Commercial foods often contain the same allergens. This is particularly obvious when looking at the list of ingredients where ingredients are often lumped together under the same heading such as 'meat and animal derivatives' or 'grain and vegetable derivatives'. This also applies to food which has been declared to be 'rich in lamb'. If this term is used, the law requires that 15 percent(!) of the meat should be lamb, but the remaining 85 percent consist of different meats.

How should I proceed once I suspect food allergy?

There are a number of different diseases which cause similar symptoms to food allergy. These include various mites, flea saliva allergies, bacterial inflammations or fungal disease. These should be checked for and, if necessary, treated by a vet.

If the suspicion of food allergy remains, an exclusion diet or elimination diet has to be followed. All the commercially available blood tests have proved to be unreliable and cannot substitute for this diet. In my view the blood tests are even counterproductive. If the result comes back negative the owner is given a false sense of security that a particular food cannot possibly be the cause of the allergy.

What is an exclusion diet?

The exclusion diet has to be composed based on the list of individual ingredients of the different foods and treats that have been fed up to this point. In doing this, it is important to understand that each ingredient represents a potential allergen. Because, as mentioned earlier, most commercial brands have similar ingredients, changing from one brand to another is not enough. The home-made diet is therefore particularly suited as an exclusion diet, if it is adhered to very strictly.

You have to choose a source of protein (mostly meat, but red kidney beans are a source of protein too) and a source of carbohydrates which the dog has never had before. This can be easily addressed if you prepare your own dog food. For example, if lamb has never been fed to your dog before, you can feed lamb. However, if you have added commercial food or treats, these would typically contain a plethora of different proteins and carbohydrates.

For this reason we often have to resort to more exotic proteins. Veal, goat, ostrich, game or rabbit are all possible, depending on the previous food habits.

Potato is usually used as a source of carbohydrate, but millet can also be used. The food should be fed raw, cooked, grilled or fried as described in previous chapters. The same applies as previously mentioned; don't make an abrupt changeover, but introduce the new food gradually over two to three days.

The most important aspect of the elimination diet is how consistently you are feeding

Choose a type of meat that your dog has never or only very rarely eaten before.

During an exclusion diet potatoes are a valuable source of carbohydrates.

exclusively those two foods you have chosen – for example game and potatoes.

Use your imagination for the preparation of homemade treats or chewy strips (meat boiled until tough, or strips of dried meat, homemade and unseasoned potato crisps, homemade burgers). Comprehensive studies have shown that over a period of three to four months a one-sided diet will not result in malnutrition. If you're dealing with a young dog, the required minerals and vitamins have to be calculated by a vet.

How long does an exclusion diet have to be followed? And what happens afterwards?

Most dogs with allergies show signs of improvement within a six-week period although for some animals this can take as long as six to ten weeks. Therefore the diet has to be followed for about six to ten weeks.

As soon as there is some improvement, a provocation with the previous food can be carried out. The timespan between the provocation and the recurrence of the symptoms can be one day to a maximum of fourteen days. You can only be certain you are dealing with a genuine food allergy if the dog shows a reaction following the provocation with the previous food (for example itching, diarrhoea). The main characteristic of an allergic reaction is that it can be triggered over and over again.

This means that the diagnosis of a food allergy can best be supported by a homemade exclusion diet, followed by a provocation. In the interest of your dog; you must be consistent!

Keeping a dog occupied during an exclusion diet

While my dog Yoda was fed his exclusion diet, I was faced with the problem of how to substitute his treats and his beloved chewable items. Every dog owner likes to give their dog a chew stick or something similar in addition to the active engagement with their dog, such as searching games for instance. During the exclusion diet no chewable items are allowed. This presents you with a problem: How do you keep your dog occupied in the house? What can I give them in order to offer an activity and a chewing treat that does not interfere with their diet? The answer is relatively simple: get one or two Kongs. These are hard rubber balls pushed together to form a cone which is hollow in the middle. You can buy them in a pet shop or on the internet. Fill the Kong with a mixture of minced meat and vegetables – both types of foods having been agreed with the vet previously – and put it in the freezer. Once the meat is frozen, you can give the Kong to the dog after allowing it to warm up enough for the dog's tongue not to get stuck to it.

The dog will lick the contents of the Kong with incredible persistence. Depending on the size of the Kong, it will take some time before the Kong is empty. The advantage is that the dog is kept busy while working for their food. Afterwards they will be visibly exhausted and have a nap. Remember to deduct the Kong ration from the daily ration. Don't worry about

To lick the contents out of a frozen Kong...

the dog's stomach getting too cold. The narrow opening of the rubber ball doesn't allow the dog to swallow any large lumps of the meat and vegetable mixture. They have to work at the snack by consistent licking. Some dogs hurl the Kong up in the air hoping

... keeps the dog occupied while enjoying a good chewing session.

that small amounts of the contents will be thrown out. Either you stop them from doing this with a firm 'No', or get the dog used to eating the Kong on the same blanket where they normally eats their bones from the outset.

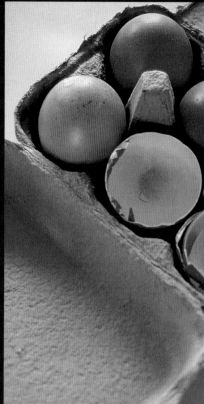

Yoda's nutritional log

In his epic drama 'Faust', the poet Goethe declared all theory to be 'grey'. For this reason I have added a practical description of a real dog's everyday feeding routine. It includes information about the dog's physical challenges and which kinds of food they should get on such occasions. The nutritional log shows how a dog's diet can (and should) be individually tailored, in order to accommodate their particular circumstances.

The dog in the cover photograph, a male Parson Russell terrier called Yoda, will serve as an example. The dog weighs just below ten kilograms, and is a very bright and alert little chap. He has been fed on a fresh food diet since the age of five months and is now, at the age of two and a half, enjoying the best of health. Yoda is a sporty dog. He does agility training once a week – a sport for humans and dogs – and he has weekly sessions at training school, learning obedience and little tricks which a dog does not need, but which provide enjoyment for both human and dog.

At home he is a quiet, calm and balanced dog. However, this is something he had to learn through me prescribing time out. While I'm working, he spends his time asleep in his basket. As soon as we're outdoors, Yoda steps on the gas. He is a ball games enthusiast. For him the main activities are running and walking, rather than wanting to catch prey.

Although Yoda only weighs just below ten kilograms, he is fed 200 grams of meat and about 400 grams of vegetables per day. Because he is a very active dog, he needs more than the daily 200 to 300 grams calculated for a dog of his weight. In the morning he gets about a third of the ration, and in the afternoon, after a big walk or training session, he gets the remaining two-thirds. His food is freshly prepared in the afternoon, and the next morning's ration is split off and stored in the fridge.

In the autumn this is an inexpensive vegetable which the dog likes too.

Saturday

Saturday is market day. The dog meat man has pure beef, mixed meats, rumen, fresh beef windpipes and chicken necks on offer. It's all looking nice and fresh. I plump for two kilograms of pure beef, a kilogram of rumen and two medium-sized pieces of windpipe, and one chicken neck.

The month is October, and it's nearly Hallowe'en. This is exactly the right time to buy a pumpkin from the vegetable stall. The planned evening meal for us humans is a tasty pumpkin and ginger soup served with lamb's lettuce.

Back home, Yoda gets a piece of chicken neck for breakfast. Yoda is keenly watching me as I divide the meat into 200 gram portions and put it in the freezer. Then I take him for a long walk along the River Elbe. He is having fun. We meet lots of other dogs who are invited to play and run along with my dog; and even the cold temperatures don't prevent my dog from taking a dip in the river. Once back home Yoda retires to his basket tired, but happy, closing his eyes immediately.

After a warming cup of tea, I tackle the pumpkin. I cut off the lid and hollow it out. I put aside about 300 grams of the firm flesh per person for the soup. The softer pumpkin flesh with the seeds removed goes straight into Yoda's vegetable blender. I prepare the lamb's lettuce for the family meal. The dog also gets a share of the salad; the roots and a handful of fresh juicy leaves. After adding a dash of linseed oil and some water the vegetables are pureed together with the meat. If I were to leave the meat in lumps, Yoda would dig out the meat and leave the vegetables behind. But he is obviously enjoying the puree. I put one-third of the portion aside for Sunday's breakfast. Later that evening Yoda also gets a beef stick, because he has a tendency to produce too much stomach acid, and will otherwise vomit yellow slime in the morning. While the dog is munching on his chew stick, I draw a scary face onto the pumpkin, and cut out eyes, nose and mouth. Thus the dog feeding routine has not just provided us with a family meal, but now we also have a Hallowe'en decoration for the sideboard, creating an autumnal atmosphere in the house.

The daily ration:
Breakfast consisting of: Chicken neck
A main meal consisting of: Pumpkin, lamb's lettuce, oil and pure beef
Bedtime treat: Beef stick

Sunday

For breakfast Yoda gets the 'leftovers' of the dinner he had the night before. Then the dog takes a nap until his lunchtime walk. Today we will drive to the forest. We have arranged to meet up with one of Yoda's canine chums, and the two dogs are running hell for leather. Every now and then they stop to have a sniff, a bit of a dig, briefly chase after a bird, initiate a friendly skirmish, and apart from that it's running and running and some more running. These Sunday walks often take a long time. As a result in the evening the dog is pretty exhausted. To suit the autumnal weather we're having a Brussels sprout bake. Before peeling the potatoes I swill them briefly under the running tap. Remaining small traces of soil sticking to the potatoes are no problem; after all a wolf would ingest a bit of soil with their food too. It won't do a dog any harm either. I boil the potato peelings separately for Yoda. A whole bag of sprouts is far too much for us. After boiling them I redirect a few sprouts into the vegetable mixer.

Many dogs are able to digest cruciferous vegetables better when they are cooked.

The daily ration:
Breakfast consisting of: Yesterday's dinner
Main meal consisting of: Potato peelings, Brussels sprouts, coconut shavings, linseed oil, rumen
Bedtime treat: Windpipe

Monday

Monday is admittedly the most boring day of the week for Yoda. After breakfast he retires to his basket once more to continue his beauty sleep. I wake him up around lunch time, and we go to the park. We usually meet plenty of dogs for playing and running together. When the weather is bad and we don't meet as many playmates, we repeat our tricks and do some obedience exercises. 'Sit', 'down' and 'stay' can never be exercised too much. Maybe Yoda will also have to search for some 'lost' treats in the grass. But this is usually all he gets on a Monday. On a Monday the terrier will usually not get more than an hour's free running time, because his owner is obliged to earn the necessary small change to keep him in meat and veg. Monday would actually be an ideal day for fasting. But because of his sensitive stomach we have the fast day on the vegetarian day. However, Yoda doesn't really appreciate vegetables on their own very much. In this respect, he is a chip off the old block, his carnivorous wolf ancestors. In order to

Together with the potato peelings, a carrot cut up small, a teaspoon of coconut shavings, oil and the defrosted rumen this will provide a firework for the pallet. I always boil cruciferous vegetables, because otherwise my dog tends to suffer from flatulence. However, many dogs are able to eat them raw. One-third of the food will be transferred to the fridge for the next breakfast. Because the Sunday walk was very extensive, Yoda gets a piece of beef windpipe as a bedtime treat. Owing to his trim figure Yoda can afford such extra-curricular feeds. If he did develop weight problems, I would of course have to deduct the weight of the windpipe from the daily 200 grams of meat.

Eggs are a delicacy for most dogs, and good for a shiny coat.

Tuesday

Monday was boring enough. This is about to change. As far as possible I normally try to arrange external appointments for a Tuesday, because on a Tuesday Yoda tends to stay with his 'dog minder'. Because I don't have a breakfast ration left over from the previous day, today he gets an old bread roll. He eats it on his fur rug, while waiting for his 'dog minder'. Normally I baulk at feeding grain to my dog, and bread rolls do contain grain. But I have never noticed any sensitivity to it in Yoda and I give him the roll without undue concern. In times of need even dry old bread tastes lovely. The hard bread roll has the useful side effect of cleaning his teeth as well.

In the evening I either pick up the completely exhausted dog from the 'dog minder', or he is brought to me. At any rate a delicious slice of leg of beef, which I got from the butcher's in the afternoon, awaits him at home.

Yoda enthusiastically carries his dinner to his fur rug and chews and chomps on his meat. The bone is too hard for his teeth. But he is

make the vegetables more attractive to him, I garnish the courgette/potato mix with an egg and a spoonful of cottage cheese.

A dash of strong smelling salmon oil will 'talk' Yoda into eating his vegetables. On occasion I let a trace of pâté or Parmesan cheese do the talking. As both are salty, I can omit the extra pinch of salt. In the evening I offer him a thin chew stick made from buffalo hide which he contentedly gnaws in his basket, but not without having chased it across the flat first.

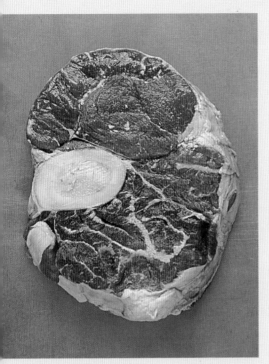

All dogs are enthusiastic about a slice of leg.

gets this gruel once a week because of his sensitive stomach. Kibbled linseed is very soothing for the stomach. For some unknown reason the normally fussy Yoda actually loves to eat this gruel... .

The daily ration:
Breakfast consisting of: Old bread roll
Main meal consisting of: Slice of leg of beef
Bedtime treat: Linseed gruel with healing earth

Wednesday

Wednesday is the absolute highlight of our week. I usually take the afternoon off (by working in the evening instead) in order to take the dog to his agility class. Because of missing out on the breakfast ration from the previous dinner, Yoda gets a Kong in the morning. For such occasions I always keep two or three Kongs filled with beef mince and mashed potatoes in the freezer.

Even as I open the freezer door the dog is standing next to me full of happy anticipation. With a grave expression he takes the heavy rubber item into his mouth and proceeds in the direction of his basket. You can hear sniffing, licking and smacking noises coming from the dog basket for at least three-quarters of an hour, depending on the size of the Kong

digging out and licking the bone marrow with keen ambition. After this challenge the inexhaustible terrier is ready for bed, slinks over to his basket and falls asleep the second he has found the right sleeping position. This often doesn't look very peaceful. His feet twitch in his dreams. He is probably busy chasing a forbidden hare.

Do you want to know what the humans had to eat today? Bread with cheese and scrambled eggs. While I was laying the table, a dish of kibbled linseeds was bubbling into a gruel on the hob. Mixed with a bit of healing earth the sleepy Yoda gets two tablespoons of this before his last 'walkies' of the day. He

A substitute for breakfast: frozen Kongs.

Vegetable peelings are ideal for the dog's dinner.

and my generosity. After this effort it's time for a little nap. Punctually at half past three we pack our things and set off to the agility training. Yoda has bags of agility talent. He

concentrates greatly on the task in hand, making it a joy to take him to classes. Concentration, however uses up a lot of energy. After an hour of agility training the dog is pretty much worn out. While the equipment is being taken down, the dogs are allowed to romp around for a change. And you don't need to tell them twice. Yoda is a proper show-off. He quickly has to try out those pieces of equipment that have not been cleared away yet. This is normally forbidden because of the risk of injury. But on many an occasion a blind eye is turned.

Our human menu plan consists of oven cheese with baguette and a large salad. While preparing salad and vegetables quite a lot comes off; the stem, the outer leaves of the green salad, the cucumber and carrot peel, the skin and the stalks of the mushrooms, the parsley stems and the slightly overripe tomato that had been forgotten in the back of the fridge. What used to end up on the compost heap is now needed for the dog's meals. The leftovers are not really waste or rubbish in the true sense. We just don't use them for human consumption. I mix yoghurt and coconut milk for our salad dressing and thicken it with a dash of lemon juice. Salt and pepper – ready! Because the dog has given his all during the afternoon, in addition to the linseed oil he also gets a good dash of coconut milk instead of coconut shavings in the vegetable blender. This restores used-up energy fast. Pureed together with the beef, this gives the

Thursday

Thursdays are usually the days when Yoda does what all dogs do; he goes for a perfectly normal walk. In the morning he gets the previous day's 'energy' meal. Due to the after-effects of Wednesday's activities Yoda sleeps right through the morning. The weather is lovely and we are thinking about a spontaneous weekend trip to the North Sea coast. The lunchtime walk takes us through the parks of Hamburg and to the beaches along the river Elbe which now, in the autumn, once more belong to dogs, walkers and kites. I can't think of anything nicer than to scamper about on a beach with the dog, throwing sticks, or simply watching him race around with his canine pals. Yoda definitely has a soft spot for big, black-haired bitches; he can spend ages running after them. With them he does not accept a 'no' when they don't want to play. He will constantly invite them, until they either briefly play with him, or make their refusal very plain indeed. The former tends to be the rule, and the usual comment from the owners is a surprised 'she never normally plays'. If there's a ball game Yoda likes to join in. He tends to be faster than the other dogs, but will give up the ball quickly when he suspects that there may be trouble afoot. On the way home we take a detour to the market. Turnips are currently cheap, and I put a large one into my shopping basket. Once back home in the warm I peel the potatoes and boil up the peelings for the dog.

After an exhausting day coconut milk restores lost energy.

dog a rich meal that will restore his energy. Tomorrow's breakfast goes in the fridge. Today's bedtime treat consists of two simple dog biscuits.

The daily ration:

Breakfast consisting of: Filled Kong

Main meal consisting of: Salad, linseed oil, coconut milk, beef

Bedtime treat: Dog biscuits

Yoda is eagerly waiting for his food bowl.

grams of beef mince in with these, and the dog is provided for. On top of this we won't come home to any shrivelled vegetable remains in the fridge. As a bedtime treat the dog gets a small piece of dried rumen.

The daily ration:
Breakfast consisting of: Yesterday's dinner
Main meal consisting of: Potato and turnip peelings, coconut shavings, siliceous earth and mixed meats
Bedtime treat: Dried rumen

I peel and dice the turnip into small pieces. Yoda's share, consisting of the washed peel, is pureed with the potato peel, coconut shavings, some siliceous earth and mixed meats. The humans of the household are having a tasty turnip stew for dinner tonight. Because we're planning a trip to the seaside for the weekend, I puree every vegetable I can find in the fridge together with oil and coconut shavings and freeze it divided up into individual portions. Upon arrival I only need to mix 200

Friday

The weather doesn't seem to want to hold; in the morning it is bucketing it down. Yoda munches his turnip–potato–meat mixture and retreats to his basket. In the afternoon I put the dog in the car and drive across town to the training school. As a puppy and young dog Yoda wasn't able to cope with car rides at all and regularly vomited. Therefore I always make sure that there is a sufficient interval between his last meal and the car ride. In addition we have trained for this: simply sitting in the stationary car, feeding treats without comment so the dog associated the car with positive things. Then I drove him around the block, then around two, three, four blocks.... Later we only used the car for trips to places where positive things could be experienced. In due

For a change these are not destined for the dog's food bowl.

the fennel offcuts pureed with carrots, salmon oil and the belly flaps. He is obviously enjoying that! Later in the evening he also gets a tasty marrow bone which he skilfully licks until it is empty.

The daily ration:
Breakfast consisting of: Yesterday's dinner
Main meal consisting of: Fennel, carrots, salmon oil, fish
Bedtime treat: Marrow bone

course he became a good passenger. Whether he has simply grown out of it or whether it was due to the training, I couldn't say.

At the dog school his 'fellow students' are almost all present already. First off, the dogs are allowed to greet each other and scamper about to their heart's content. After that things proceed in a more orderly fashion, just as one would expect from a training class with the title 'sport and fun'. Yoda is usually completely worn out after so much concentration. In addition we have to drive across the whole of town for an hour. We add a little detour to the fishmonger. There I buy fresh mackerel for us humans. I get fish belly flaps for the dog at a very good price. The greengrocer has fennel and carrots on offer. I make a purchase. In the evening we're having mackerel filets with pasta and a fennel sauce. The dog gets

Appendix

Nutritional table for meat and fish

Product (in 100 g)	Protein in g	Fat in g	Calcium in mg	Phosphorus in mg	Energy in kJ
Beef heart			2	173	590
Beef liver	19.5	3.38	6.1	352	547
Beef rumen, green	19	5.0	120	130	394
Beef windpipe			40	70	428
Beef omasum	14	5.0	90	80	540
Beef (best rib)	20.6	8.05	4.4	149	647
Beef (pure muscle)	22.0	1.9	5.7	190	455
Beef (tail section)	21.5	2.35	3.8	195	452
Chicken	18.5	20.3	11	180	1066
Hare	21.6	3.01	14	210	479
Herring (Baltic Sea)	18.1	9.60	68	210	646
Horsemeat	20.6	2.67	9.2	216	456
Lamb (pure muscle)	20.8	3.7	3	-	491
Mackerel	18.7	11.9	12	244	758
Mutton (fillet)	20.4	3.41	12	162	473
Mutton (leg)	18.0	18	10	213	972
Pike	18.4	0.85	32	225	344
Plaice	17.1	1.90	61	198	361
Pollock	18.3	0.90	14	300	344
Rabbit (with bones)	20.8	7.62	14	216	636
Redfish	18.2	3.61	22	201	443
Salmon	19.9	13.6	15	253	842
Trout	19.5	2.73	12	245	433
Tuna	21.5	15.50	40	400	939
Veal (knuckle with bone)	21.2	2.66	15	195	459
Veal (pure muscle)	21.3	0.81	13	198	3,92
Venison (leg)	21.4	1.25	5	220	410

Nutritional table for vegetables

Product (in 100 g)	Protein in g	Fat in g	Calcium in mg	Phosphorus in mg	Energy in kJ
Asparagus	1.91	0.16	26	45	75
Beetroot	1.08	-	-	29	156
Broccoli	3.54	0.20	58	65	117
Brussels sprouts	4.45	0.34	33	84	151
Carrots	0.98	0.20	37	35	109
Cauliflower	2.46	0.28	21	52	95
Celery	1.55	0.33	50	74	77
Chicory	1.27	0.18	26	26	70
Courgettes	1.89	0.29	25	29	81
Cress	4.20	0.70	214	38	139
Cucumber	0.60	0.20	16	17	52
Dandelion leaves	2.87	0.62	165	67	113
Fennel	2.43	0.30	109	51	101
Kohlrabi	1.94	0.16	64	50	104
Lamb's lettuce	1.84	0.36	35	49	58
Lettuce	1.22	0.22	22	23	49
Mushrooms	4.11	0.25	11	125	67
Parsley, leaf	4.43	0.36	179	87	214
Potatoes	2.04	0.11	6.4	50	298
Pumpkin	1.10	0.13	22	44	104
Rocket	2.60	0.70	160	-	62
Sauerkraut	1.52	0.31	48	43	71
Savoy cabbage	2.78	0.32	64	56	109
Sorrel	3.19	0.36	58	51	87
Spinach	3.20	0.30	116	48	69.9
Sweetcorn	3.28	1.23	2.2	83	369
Swiss chard	2.13	0.28	103	39	58

Nutritional table for fruit

Product (in 100 g)	Protein in g	Fat in g	Calcium in mg	Phosphorus in mg	Energy in kJ
Apples	1.00	0.70	12	28	225
Apricots	0.90	0.13	16	21	183
Bananas	1.15	0.18	7	23	374
Blackberries	1.20	1.00	44	30	186
Blueberries	0.60	0.60	10	13	153
Cherries	0.90	0.30	17	23	265
Cranberries	0.28	0.53	14	9.7	148
Kiwifruit	1.00	0.63	38	31	215
Mandarins	0.70	0.30	33	20	195
Mango	0.60	0.45	12	13	243
Oranges	1.00	0.20	40	20	179
Peaches	0.76	0.11	6.3	21	176
Pears	1.00	0.70	12	28	225
Pineapple	0.46	0.15	12	17	69
Plums	0.60	0.17	8.3	17	205
Raspberries	1.30	0.30	40	44	143
Redcurrants	1.13	0.20	29	27	139
Strawberries	0.82	0.40	21	26	136
Watermelon	0.60	0.20	7.3	9.2	159
Yellow plum	0.73	0.20	12	33	269

Nutritional table for other foods

Product (in 100 g)	Protein in g	Fat in g	Calcium in mg	Phosphorus in mg	Energy in kJ
Bread roll	8.96	1.90	27	102	1.155
Chicken egg	12.8	11.30	54	214	570
Coconut	4.63	36.50	20	94	1.498
Cottage cheese	12.1	4.30	95	150	428
Crispbread	10.10	1.40	55	301	1.335
French toast	9.9	4.3	42	132	1.558
Honey (flower honey)	0.38	-	5.9	4.9	1.283
Linseed	28.80	30.90	198	662	1.558
Oils (average)	-	100	-	-	3.700
Pasta, boiled	4.30	0.91	9.0	62	399
Quark, 20% fat	12.2	5.10	85	165	457
Rice, boiled	2.10	0.16	3,0	36	359
Yoghurt, 3.5% fat	3.80	3.75	120	92	293

Literature

MacDonald, Carina Beth
Raw Dog Food: Making it Work for You and
Your Dog. Dogwise Publishing, 2003

Martin, Ann N.
Protect your Pet.
New Sage Press, 2001

Martin, Ann N.
Food Pets Die for.
New Sage Press, 1997

O'Grady, Patricia
Woofing it Down: The Quick & Easy Guide
to Making Healthy Dog Food at Home.
Authorhouse, 2007

Roberts, Donna Twichell
The Good Food Cookbook for Dogs:
50 Home-Cooked Recipes for the Health and
Happiness of Your Canine Companion.
Crestline, 2009

Thanks

I would like to thank everybody from the bottom of my heart who has helped to make this book a success!

My particular thanks to Dr Vet Monika Linek for the contribution 'Food allergies and food intolerances'.

I experienced some very special and straight-forward assistance from Meike Weiland, Claudia Kopp-Ulrich (Hundeschule Ulrich, Freiburg) and Franziska Bokeloh.

For this I thank you all!